Printed in Victoria, BC, Canada

Note for Librarians: a cataloguing record for this book that includes Dewey Decimal Classification and US Library of Congress numbers is available from the Library and Archives of Canada. The complete cataloguing record can be obtained from their online database at:
www.collectionscanada.ca/amicus/index-e.html

ISBN 1-4120-5005-7

TRAFFORD

Offices in Canada, USA, Ireland, UK and Spain

This book was published on-demand in cooperation with Trafford Publishing. On-demand publishing is a unique process and service of making a book available for retail sale to the public taking advantage of on-demand manufacturing and Internet marketing. On-demand publishing includes promotions, retail sales, manufacturing, order fulfilment, accounting and collecting royalties on behalf of the author.

Book sales for North America and international:

Trafford Publishing, 6E–2333 Government St.,

Victoria, BC v8t 4p4 CANADA

phone 250 383 6864 (toll-free 1 888 232 4444)

fax 250 383 6804; email to orders@trafford.com

Book sales in Europe:

Trafford Publishing (uk) Ltd., Enterprise House, Wistaston Road Business Centre,

Wistaston Road, Crewe, Cheshire cw2 7rp UNITED KINGDOM

phone 01270 251 396 (local rate 0845 230 9601)

facsimile 01270 254 983; orders.uk@trafford.com

Order online at:
www.trafford.com/robots/04-2813.html

10 9 8 7 6 5 4 3

THE FOURTH MYSTERY DRAMA

THE SOULS AWAKENING

....

A Series of Soul and Spiritual Events
In Dramatic Scenes

....

by

Rudolf Steiner

THE MODERN SPIRIT PRESS
and

TRAFFORD

The stage directions in this drama are from the point of view of the audience

The Fourth Mystery Drama (The Souls Awakening) is a translation from the German of **Der Seelen Erwachen**. This translation follows the pagination and lineation (with a few minor adjustments necessary for this English printing) of the current German hardback (not paperback) edition 1998. In German it is published together with the three other Mystery Dramas as **Vier Mysteriendramen** and may be obtained from Rudolf Steiner Verlag, Dornach, Switzerland, (copyright 1956 by Rudolf Steiner Nachlassverwaltung, Dornach) under the ISBN 3727401400 or ISBN 3727457120 (pocket hardback). This translation has taken into account the first German edition of 1913, the apparent last German edition (1922) during Rudolf Steiner's lifetime, the German editions of 1935, 1948, 1981, as well as 1998.

This drama has been previously translated and published in English under the titles: **The Soul's Awakening, The Souls' Awakening**.

CHARACTERS, FIGURES AND EVENTS

The series of soul and spiritual events presented in **The Souls Awakening** are to be thought of as following about one year after those depicted in my previously appearing drama, **The Guardian of the Threshold**.

For the events in **The Souls Awakening**, the following persons and beings come under consideration:

I. **The Bearers of the Spiritual Element:**
    1. *Benedictus*, the personality in whom a number of his "pupils" see the knower of deep spiritual relationships. (In my previous soul sketches, **Initiation: The Gate of Consecration** and **The Soul's Testing**, he is portrayed as the leader of the "Sun Temple". In him comes to expression, in **The Guardian of the Threshold**, the spiritual stream that wants to put a living, present-day, spiritualized cultural life in place of the merely traditional type as preserved by the "Fellowship of Mystics" met with in that play.) In **The Souls Awakening**, Benedictus is no longer to be thought of as simply standing over his pupils, rather as woven into their soul experiences with his own soul destiny.
    2. *Hilary* True-to-God <Hilarius Gottgetreu>. The knower of traditional spiritual life that with him is connected with his own spirit experiences. (The same individuality portrayed in my previously appearing soul sketch, **The Soul's Testing**, as the Grand Master of a "mystic brotherhood".)
    3. *The Office Manager* of Hilary True-to-God. (The same personality appearing as Frederick Mind <Friedrich Geist> in **The Guardian of the Threshold**.)

II. **The Bearers of the Element of Devotion:**
    1. *Magnus Bellicosus*, (Called Germanus <German> in **Initiation: The Gate of Consecration**. In **The Soul's Testing** and in **The Guardian of the Threshold**, Preceptor of a "mystic brotherhood.")

2. *Albert Torquatus.* (Called "Theodosius" in **Initiation: The Gate of Consecration**. In **The Soul's Testing**, the same individuality appears as First Master of Ceremonies of the therein depicted "mystic brotherhood".)

3. Professor *Capesius.* (In **The Soul's Testing** his personality appears as the First Preceptor.)

4. *Felix Bald* <Balde>. (In **Initiation: The Gate of Consecration** as bearer of a certain Nature mysticism; here in **The Souls Awakening**, the bearer of subjective mysticism. The individuality Felix Bald appears as "Joseph Keen" in **The Soul's Testing**.)

III. **The Bearers of the Will Element:**

1. *Romanus* (is here reintroduced under the name used for him in **Initiation: The Gate of Consecration** because this corresponds more with the inner individuality to which he has worked his way through during the years lying between **Initiation: The Gate of Consecration**, and **The Souls Awakening**. In **The Guardian of the Threshold**, the name (Frederick Trustworthy <Friederick Trautmann>) used for him is to be thought of as his name in the outer world. He is introduced with that name there, because with his inner life he has only a limited significance within the series of events appearing there. His individuality appears in **The Soul's Testing** as the Second Master of Ceremonies of the medieval "mystic brotherhood".)

2. *Doctor Strader.* (Doctor of Science/Engineering. His individuality appears in **The Soul's Testing** as "Simon the Jew".)

3. *The Nurse* of Doctor Strader. (Is the same personality who in **The Guardian of the Threshold** was named Maria Faithful <Maria Treufels>. In **Initiation: The Gate of Consecration** she is called "The Other Maria" because the imaginative knowledge of Johannes Thomasius fashions the imagination of certain Rulers of Nature in her likeness. Her individuality appears in **The Soul's Testing** as "Bertha", the daughter of the Keens.)

4. *Mrs. Bald* <Balde>. (Her individuality appears in **The Soul's Testing** as "Mrs. Keen".)

IV. The Bearers of the Soul Element:

1. *Maria* (Her individuality appears in **The Soul's Testing** as the "Monk".)
2. *Johannes Thomasius* (His individuality appears in **The Soul's Testing** as "Thomas".)
3. *The Wife of Hilary* True-to-God.

V. Beings from the Spirit World:

1. Lucifer
2. Ahriman
3. Gnomes
4. Sylphs

VI. Beings of the Human Spiritual Element:

1. Philia
2. Astrid ⎱ spiritual beings who mediate
3. Luna ⎰ the connection of the human soul forces with the cosmos
4. The Other Philia, the bearer of the element of love in the world the spiritual personality belongs to.
5. The Soul of Theodora. (Her individuality appears in **The Soul's Testing** as "Cecilia" <Cäcilia>, the Keen's foster daughter and sister of "Thomas", who presents the individuality of Johannes Thomasius.)
6. The Guardian of the Threshold.
7. The Double of Johannes Thomasius
8. The Spirit of Johannes Thomasius's Youth
9. The Soul of "Renard Fox" <Ferdinand Reinecke> in the realm of Ahriman: Scene 12 (only appears as "Renard Fox" in **The Guardian of the Threshold**.)

VII:

The personalities of Benedictus and Maria are also introduced as experiences in thought, specifically, in the Second Scene as those by Johannes Thomasius, in the Third Scene as those by Strader. In the Tenth Scene, Maria alone is introduced as an experience in thought by Johannes Thomasius.

VIII:

The individualities of Benedictus, Hilary True-to-God, Magnus Bellicosus, Albert Torquatus, Strader, Capesius, Felix Bald, Mrs. Bald, Romanus, Maria, Johannes Thomasius and Theodora appear in the domain of the spirit (in the Fifth and Sixth Scenes of **The Souls Awakening**) as "souls", and in the Temple (of the Seventh and Eighth Scenes of **The Souls Awakening**) as personalities of a far distant past.

In regard to **The Souls Awakening**, a remark also needs to be made similar to that for the preceeding soul sketches. Neither the soul and spiritual series of events, nor the spiritual beings are intended as simply symbolical or allegorical. For whoever wants to take them in that way, the real beings of the spiritual world remain far off.

In the presentations of the experiences in thought as well (Second, Third and Tenth Scenes), nothing purely symbolic is portrayed, rather real soul experiences which, for a person taking part in the spiritual world, are as real as persons or events in the sense world. For such a person, **The Souls Awakening** portrays a thoroughly "realistic" soul sketch. If the matter had to do with symbolism or allegory, I quite certainly would have left these portrayals out.

In response to various questions, I this time, too, began the attempt to add in a few clarifications as "additional remarks" to this "soul sketch". As formerly, I this time, too, suppressed them. It goes against the grain to add something like that to a sketch supposed to speak for itself. That kind of abstraction could play no role at the conception or working out of the sketch; they would only have had a disturbing effect there. The spiritual reality reproduced here is placed before the soul with just the same necessity as the things of physical perception are. In the nature of things, a picture from spirit perception by healthy spiritual vision is related to its beings and events differently than the perception of the physical world is to its respective beings and events. On the other hand, it must be said that the manner in which a series of spiritual events are placed before the perceiving soul contains within itself both the arrangement and the composition of such a sketch.

Special mention should be made here that the musical contributions for the performances of the four Dramas stem from Adolf Arenson.

Munich, August, 1913

SCENE ONE

Hilary's counting room. Furnished in a not all too new style. We may presume Hilary is the owner of some kind of lumber or woodworking mill. Office Manager and Secretary in conversation; Hilary; later Strader. °

SECRETARY:

> And also our customers in Georgetown
> Make it clear they're dissatisfied.

OFFICE MANAGER:

> Even those now; that's really pitiful
> And always the same reasons; one can see
> How painful these good customers find it
> To have to break with Hilary.

SECRETARY:

> That we're letting punctuality slip,
> That our workmanship doesn't measure up
> To the performance of other firms in our field,
> That's what they're writing us; I hear
> The same thing continually on my business trips.
> The good name of the company as it was passed on
> To us from Hilary's forefathers and which
> We've been able to improve, is going down hill.
> The opinion is now going round
> Hilary is deluded by dreamers and visionaries
> And the rapturous mood now gripping him robs him
> Of that attention to detail that previously bestowed
> It's unique, world-renowned special character
> On each and every piece of work by the company.
> As great a number as were once our praisers,
> Are now as certain complainers about our work.

OFFICE MANAGER:

For quite a while now I've been aware of how
Hilary lets himself be driven into error by people
Who are striving for 'unusual' mental abilities.
His soul always was inclined to such impulses,
But earlier he knew enough to hold them apart
From the production that pays the day.
(Hilary True-to-God enters the room.)

OFFICE MANAGER:

I think maybe it's time to speak
With the boss alone for a bit.
(The secretary leaves the room.)

OFFICE MANGER:

Because of my concern, I'd like to take
This opportunity to ask for a serious talk.

HILARY:

What is it that's causing my advisor concern?

OFFICE MANAGER:

Many recent incidents are clearly indicating
The quality of our work is falling off more and more
And that we're no longer producing as we should.
Increasingly, voices are complaining about
How our performance is decreasing in value
And other companies are overtaking our position.
Also, our well-known punctuality of old is missed
By many, and with rights. Very soon now our best
Customers won't be satisfied with Hilary any more.

HILARY:

I've been very well aware of this for some time now,

But frankly, it leaves me quite unconcerned.
Nevertheless, to go over the situation
Is definitely needful, for you haven't
Simply helped me as an employee in my firm,
You've always stood by me as a true friend.
So now you're going to hear quite plainly
What I've already hinted at often enough.
Whoever wants to create the new must be able
To calmly experience the decline of the old.
I don't want to manage the business in the future
The way it's been done up till now.
Letting profit flow in only the most confined circuit,
And simply thoughtlessly delivering products of work
To the daily markets of our earthy life
Totally unconcerned about what'll become of them –
That seems to me to be unworthy ever since I've
Learned what a noble form work can take on when
Spiritually oriented people put their stamp on it.
From now on, Thomasius, as artist,
Is going to direct the production site
I intend to build for him in the vicinity.
Then what we manage to produce mechanically
Will be artistically fashioned by his spirit,
And thus what is useful and bears noble beauty
Will be delivered up for the people's daily needs.
Craftsmanship will be united with art,
Everyday life permeated with good taste.
I'll thus add to the dead physical form,
As something that does seem to me to be our work,
The soul, which first bestows meaning on it. °

OFFICE MANAGER (*after prolonged pondering*):
This plan for such marvellous creating °
Is not appropriate to the spirit of our times;

All production today must still strictly strive
For perfection within the most confined circuit.
Those powers in life impersonally letting
The part efficiently stream over into the whole
Unthinkingly give to each member the value
Our own wisdom is not yet able to give it; °
And even if this didn't stand in your way,
Still your intentions would be in vain;
For to believe you can find the person who can
Realize this plan you've already thought out –
That I'm just not capable of.

HILARY:

My friend, you know I don't follow dreams.
How could I have ever set such high goals
If good fortune hadn't brought me the man
Who is to carry out what I'm striving for;
And I have to wonder your eye
Hasn't noticed that man in Strader.
One who has got to know the true nature of his spirit °
And has a sense for our highest human obligations
Surely shouldn't be called a dreamer
When he senses it as his duty
To create a field of work for such a man.

OFFICE MANAGER *(after he has shown some astonishment)*:

In Strader I'm supposed to see such a spirit!
Hasn't it been demonstrated clearly enough with him
How the human mind is capable of blinding itself
When a sense for the realities fails it.
That his mechanism has spirit light to thank
As its source – that can't be doubted,
And when at last it can be realized,
All the benefits will certainly flow from it

Strader can already believe are so near;
But it's going to remain a model for a long time yet
Since at present the forces still lie hidden
That could first create the reality for him.
It saddens me you could think
Good may come about if you entrust your work
To this man who has suffered such shipwreck
With his own boldly thoughtout invention.
It certainly did lead his spirit to those heights
That are always enticing our human soul;
Heights, however, it should only climb
When the right forces are its own.

HILARY:

Still, that you praise the spirit of this man
While seeking reasons to condemn him
Testifies quite especially to his worth.
According to your own words, it's not due to him
His creation has not been accorded success.
So he is quite certainly at the right place here
Within our circle; nothing from outside will
Now be able to direct itself against his spirit.

OFFICE MANAGER:

And even if I now try, through an inner effort
Against everything I've just spoken,
To put myself into your type of thinking,
Still other things force me into opposition.
Who will value your performance in the future,
And who'll show you sufficient understanding
They'll make use of your workmanship?
What possessions you have will be eaten up
By the time the work first begins,
Then it won't be possible to take it any further.

HILARY:

It's certainly clear to me that my plans
Would have to be seen as incomplete
If an understanding were not first created
For this new style and way of working.
What Strader, what Thomasius are working on,
That will be brought to completion at the site
I shall found to foster spiritual knowledge.
What Benedictus, what Capesius
And what Maria will there make known,
That should show pathways to the human spirit
In such a manner that its own need to permeate
Sense existence with spirit revelation will increase.

OFFICE MANAGER:

You're certainly going to make that small circle
Living for itself far from worldly existence happy.
You're closing yourselves off from real human life.
With this, you want to wipe out the sense of self,
Yet at your new place, you'll but nurture it.

HILARY:

You seem to think that in a dream I'm thoughtlessly
Denying the practical skills that have furnished me
My life. I would be acting like that
If for one second I understood success in your sense.
What seems worthwhile to me may well go awry,
But even if the whole world simply despised it
And it therefore had to collapse in upon itself,
Still, it would have been placed once upon the earth
By human souls as an archetypal model.
It would work on spiritually in life
Even when not preserved in sense appearance.
In it, part of the force would have been created

That will eventually have to lead to the marriage
Of spiritual goals and physical deeds.
So proclaims the science of the spirit.

OFFICE MANAGER:

As an employee in your factory with a sense of duty
I wanted to speak about what seemed needful,
But your attitude also gives me the right
To open myself as friend to friend.
While working at your side, I've felt impelled
For many years to seek knowledge of those things
You've dedicated yourself to
And sacrificed many of your forces to.
I could only find instruction in the writings
That sought to reveal that spiritual knowledge. –
Even if those worlds I then saw myself
Directed to were closed to me,
Still, I was capable of intuitively imagining how
People devoted in faith to that approach to the
Spirit would have to feel quite in harmony with it.
Through my own rooting around, I confirmed
What many who know this area of research
Clearly describe as a peculiar phenomenon of souls
Who come to feel at home in the spirit domain.
Above all, it seems to me significant that despite
Their care, such souls don't know enough to separate
Delusion from reality when in the natural course
Of things they're supposed to find their way back
Again to earthly existence from the spirit heights. –
At that point, images emerge from the spirit world
Where they are experiencing themselves that prevent
A correct view of physical existence for their soul
And deceptively confuse the power of judgement
A person needs for their earthly life.

HILARY:

>   What you're trying to put forward as objection
>   Only strengthens me, since it clearly shows
>   That in you I may now know one more trusted
>   Individual for my future research work.
>   How was I ever to have guessed up to now
>   The type of soul willing to unite
>   With me for this work is well known to you.
>   You know some of the dangers threatening them,
>   So their deeds will also demonstrate to you
>   They do know the paths which will safeguard them.
>   The situation will soon be well understood by you,
>   And in future, as well, I'll find in you
>   The adviser I cannot do without.

OFFICE MANAGER:

>   I cannot direct my energy to deeds
>   Where I don't know how they'll take effect.
>   It seems to me the people you've entrusted
>   Yourself to have truly fallen into the delusion
>   I've just spoken of, and such a delusion will
>   Also tempt others who might wish to listen to them.
>   It drowns out a conscious, goal-oriented thinking.
>   If you intend to build up such activities
>   On foundations that rest for their support
>   On our earthly life, you'll find me at your side
>   Advising you for all times to come;
>   But your new ways are not for me.

HILARY:

>   By your refusal, you're endangering this work
>   That is intended to serve spiritual goals,
>   For without your advice, I'll be lamed.
>   Consider further, that a solemn duty arises

When destiny gives us a sign
Like the one quite clearly recognizable to me
By the presence of these people.

OFFICE MANAGER:

The more you speak to me like this,
The more it is simply made clear
You've long fallen into error unawares.
You think you're rendering service to humanity;
In truth, you're now only serving this circle,
Which through your support can devote itself
For a short while longer to its spirit dream.
A bustle of activity will soon unfold itself here
The spirit is indeed ordering *these* souls to do °
But which will nevertheless be shown to be a mirage °
Which will eat up the fruits of our past labors.

HILARY:

If you won't extend me your hand now,
The future must stand clouded before my soul.
(Dr. Strader enters from the right.)
My good Strader, I've been expecting you.
It's just come out that it might be better
If we were to discuss a few significant things now
And only make the outing at a later time. °
My old friend here has just confided to me what
We're beginning doesn't seem advantageous to him.
So now let the man speak for himself
Who has pledged his spirit to our work.
At this point, much depends upon how individuals
Can find each other within their souls,
Which are like different worlds
Confronting one another but which
When united are to create great things.

STRADER:

> So does the trusted assistant of Hilary
> Not wish to commit himself to this hopeful project
> The wisdom of our friend makes possible?
> Yet this plan will now only be able to succeed
> When the good old-fashioned ways of living life
> Wisely want to join with future goals.

OFFICE MANAGER:

> It's not that I want to simply keep myself apart;
> I would also like to show my good friend
> The pointlessness of this undertaking.

STRADER:

> It doesn't surprise me a plan bearing
> "Strader" on it appears unsuitable to you.
> I had to see an important project come to nought,
> Because for our age the forces are still hidden that
> Bring what is well thought-out to material effect.
> You know I have to thank spiritual illumination
> For what did prove itself but couldn't come to life.
> This testifies against my powers of judgement
> And also tends to kill all belief our spirit
> Harbors the well-springs of real earthly creation.
> - - - - - - - - - -
> And it will be difficult to prove
> Such experience gives me the forces
> To avoid that error in this second case.
> I had to err then so reality's rocky cliffs
> Could be avoided with safety this time ...
> - - - - - - - - - -
> Yet it *is* understandable you doubt this.
> Your sort of spirit in particular must find
> Our manner of work promises but little.

- - - - - - - - - -
They praise you especially for how judiciously you
Participate in all of our social and cultural life
And also devote helpful time and forces to it;
But they also say you want to have daily production
Kept separate in the strictest manner
From all spiritual striving wanting to work
Creatively within our soul life from our own forces.
You would rather regard that as simply the content
Of times not filled out by work. To join what
Spirit brings about in spirit to projects
Arising within sense appearance is the goal
Of that spiritual stream quite clearly showing
Me the course of development life is taking.

OFFICE MANAGER:

As long as spirit offers up to spirit
Solely what it can produce by independent creating,
It raises souls up to a human worthiness
Giving them meaning in their earthly existence;
But when it also experiences existence in itself
And even wants to master still other existences,
Then it approaches domains where delusion
Can often become dangerous for the truth.
That through my efforts with spiritual things
Such a knowledge has been revealed to me
Confirms me in my attitude today, and
Not what you may regard as my heart's inclination,
Being led on by my reputation.

STRADER:

So in you an error in spiritual knowledge
Is now placed in hostility over against my views.
Now the difficulties will increase.

To join together for a project with people
Who previously had let themselves be instructed
From nature and life by a sense for their existence
Would be quite easy for the spirit researcher to do,
But when thoughts that are to be created
From spirit well-springs have to be united
With reluctance to others of the same origin,
Harmony is only seldom to be hoped for.
- - - - - - - - - -

- - - - - - - - - -

(After some quiet pondering.)

Yet what must happen, will happen.
Renewed testing of my plans will – – –
Perhaps change the opinion that
Had to form in you with this first consideration.

(The curtain falls while all three are lost in thought.)

SCENE TWO

A mountain landscape; in the background, Hilary's house, which is to be thought of as near the mill, although the mill itself is not visible. A waterfall on the right side. To begin with, Johannes; not visible to him, Capesius.

JOHANNES:

    This taciturn existence of towered forms
    Crowds space full sculpting its broad riddles;
    Not with questioning agony does it deaden the souls
    Living in blessedness who wish not to understand,
    Wish simply to behold this revelation of existence.
    Around these rocky cliffs of this light's weaving,
    The mute existence of barren surfaces here,
    The wilderness, green dawning into blue there;
    Such is the world in which Johannes's soul,
    Weaving pictures of the future, wishes to linger.
    - - - - - - - - - -
    - - - - - - - - - -

    Johannes's soul is to experience within itself
    The depths and the widths of this world,
    And Creating Powers are to set free for this soul
    The force that can make known to human hearts
    World magic as artistically transfigured appearance.
    - - - - - - - - - -

    Yet never would Johannes be capable of this
    If his soul forces were not lovingly awakened
    By Maria through her mild soul warmth.
    I must praise the wise guidance of destiny
    That has brought me so near this person.
    How short, indeed, the time since I have
    Known her at my side; how these few weeks
    Have already inwardly bound my soul

To her soul in a life-long union.
She lives as spirit within me, even when she's far;
She thinks in my thinking when I summon up
Before my soul what my willing strives towards.
(Maria appears as a thought of Johannes's.)

JOHANNES *(continuing on)*:
Maria, here before me? but *how* has she? –
She's not allowed to show herself like this before me;
This spiritually stern countenance – this dignity
Making earthly feelings shiver – Johannes –
He does not wish to – he cannot behold Maria
Near him like this – this cannot possibly
Be the Maria whom the wise Powers guided to me
In their mild dispensation of my destiny.
(Maria disappears from Johannes's vision.)
Where is the Maria who loved Johannes
Before she had transformed his soul
And led it onto cold spirit heights?
- - - - - - - - - -

But also Johannes, who loved Maria,
Where then is he? – he was here just now –
I can no longer see the Johannes who so
Blissfully restored me to myself – the past cannot,
Should not, cruelly rob me of him!
(Maria again becomes visible to Johannes's vision.)

MARIA:
Maria, as you wish to behold her,
She is not in those worlds where truth shines out.
Seduced by the soul's delusion, Johannes's spirit is
Now weaving in realms of deception; – free yourself
From the Powers of Desire tempting you.
I am experiencing the storm in your soul within me;

It is robbing me of the tranquility I need.
It's not Johannes who is directing
Such a storm into my soul; it's a being
He already overcame within himself ages ago.
It now flits through spirit widths as delusion –
Recognize it, and it will disperse into nothingness.

JOHANNES:

This is Maria as she truly is,
And she is speaking about Johannes
As he really does appear at times to himself.
He long ago raised himself to an existence other
Than what this phantasmagorical play of dreams
Now paints for me because in lazy tranquility
I wish to let my soul comfortably doze within itself.
But *not yet* does that existence embrace my being.
I can still escape it – and right now wish to. –
It often calls me to it, with its forces
It then wants to win me over totally for itself, – –
Yet it drives me to free myself from it.
For many years it has filled
My soul depths with spirit existence,
And yet – I do not now wish to know of it within me.
- - - - - - - - - -
You foreign being within Johannes's soul,
Leave me – give me myself as I once was
Before you showed yourself as active within me. – –
(*Benedictus appears at Maria's side; similarly as a thought of
Johannes's.*)

BENEDICTIS:

Johannes, heed the warning of your soul;
The one imbuing you with spirit, who has emerged

417

As the primary ruling power of your being,
He must reign faithfully by your side
And demand you create in a human way
The forces of his being within your willing.
He must work hidden within your self
So one day you may become what you know now
Is the distant future goal of your own being.
You should bear your own cares through life
Firmly closed off within your inner soul.
You yourself will only win yourself if you bravely
Will to let yourself be ever more possessed by him.

MARIA *(looked on as thought by Johannes)*:

My holy solemn vow rays forth the force
That shall preserve for you what you have won.
You will find me in those cold fields of ice
Where spirits must themselves create their light
When dark regions lame the forces of their life. – –
Seek me in those cosmic foundations where souls
Must battle to win what the gods feel by mean of °
The victories that from nothingness wrest existence;
But never seek me in that realm of shades
Where a lived-out soul-life obtains by artifice
A fleeting existence from an illusory being,
And phantasmagorical dream-plays cocoon the spirit,
Because in enjoyment it wishes to forget itself,
And *seriousness* might seem unsettling to it.
(Benedictus and Maria disappear.)

JOHANNES:

She speaks of delusion – – – –
– – – – yet how beautiful is this delusion.
He lives; Johannes feels his self within him,
He also feels Maria's nearness within him. – –

Johannes does not want to know how the spirit
Solves riddles in the soul's dark depths;
But he does want to create, want to work as artist.
So let remain hidden from him what in him would
Consciously like to look only on cosmic heights.

- - - - - - - - - -

(*He sinks into further reflections:*)
(*Capesius stands up from his seat; rouses himself as if from deep reflection.*)

CAPESIUS:

Was I not clearly experiencing within my own soul
What is being created as images of longing
Within Johannes, who is so dreamily reflecting?
Thoughts flamed up within me that weren't
From me – – which only he could have produced.
His soul's existence was living within mine. – –
I saw him grown young, how he beheld himself
By means of spirit delusion and wantonly
Reviled the ripened fruits of his own spirit. – –

- - - - - - - - - -

But how! – why do I experience this now?
For only seldom may spirit searchers
Behold within themselves another soul existence! –

- - - - - - - - - -

From Benedictus I have often heard how only
Those are capable of doing this – for a short time –
Who are chosen by the grace of destiny
In order to be raised *one* step higher
On the spirit path. – – May I so understand
What has come to me at this moment?
What seldom – truly only – is *allowed* to happen;
For it would be terrible if the seer could eavesdrop
At any time on the inner existence of other souls.

- - - - - - - - - -
- - - - - - - - - -

Whether I beheld the truth – – whether a delusion
Let me dream about another soul's existence?
This I must find out from Johannes himself.
(Capesius approaches Johannes and is only now noticed by the latter.)

JOHANNES:

Capesius – I thought you far from here!

CAPESIUS:

But my soul felt itself close to you.

JOHANNES:

Close to me – just now – surely not!

CAPESIUS:

Why then do you shudder at these words?

JOHANNES:

Oh no, I'm not shuddering – – –
(At this moment Maria enters; this makes it possible that the next words of Johannes as well as those of Capesius can be spoken to themselves.)

JOHANNES *(to himself)*:

– – – His glance, it truly does
Pierce into the depths of my soul.

CAPESIUS *(to himself)*:

His shuddering shows me I saw truly.
(Capesius now turns to Maria.)
Maria, you appear at just the right moment.

Perhaps your words will bring a solution
To this difficult problem so oppressing me!

MARIA:

Not you – I thought to find Johannes here.
Intuition led me to seek the burden of the problem
With him – you, however, I imagined satisfied,
Devoted to the beautiful goal of that project
Hilary wants to make possible for us.

CAPESIUS:

That goal – what's it to me – it's now disturbing me.

MARIA:

It's disturbing you? – Didn't you express delight,
Since just such a development was what you hoped for?

CAPESIUS:

What I've experienced at this destiny-laden moment
Has completely changed my soul direction; *any* earthly
Activity will rob me of clairvoyant forces now awoken.

MARIA:

Those permitted to walk the spirit pathways
Experience there the hint of many a sign of destiny. –
They are supposed to follow them along soul paths,
But they can't have been rightly interpreted
If they disturb one's true earthly duties.
*(Capesius sits, falling into a short reflection; while that is
happening, Maria experiences the appearance of Lucifer.)*

LUCIFER:

Your efforts will bring you little reward.
Within his heart are aroused the forces

Opening the gates of his soul to me.
Maria – direct your clairvoyant force
Into his soul depths – behold there
How with spirit wings he frees himself
From your love-warmed earthly work.
(Lucifer remains in the landscape.)
(Maria turns herself somewhat more directly towards Capesius in order to awaken him out of his reflections, from which, however, at the same instant, he is also aroused as if by himself.)

MARIA:

If Johannes were to feel disturbed on his spirit
Pathway by the nature of his duties, that wouldn't
Be right – although it would seem understandable:
He will have to do things in external service;
But you are supposed to make known spirit teachings
And thus not step outside your own soul's circle.

CAPESIUS:

Far more than when it creates outer works,
The spirit force can become lost in words.
Words compel one to understand what was beheld,
Yet these concepts are hostile to clairvoyant forces.
I was allowed to behold a spirit experience that
Could only show itself to my eye because the soul
That opened really is close to my earthly person,
Yet has *never* been completely understood by it. –
Should my experience prove true, nothing will
Be able to bind me to this earthly work
Since I will then have to feel
Exalted Powers are indicating to my soul
Goals other than those Hilary has marked out for it.
(He places himself before Johannes.)

Johannes, tell me frankly, didn't you just now,
When you were fully lost in your reflections,
Experience old lived-out soul desires
As your own present self within you.

JOHANNES:

Can my spirit's confusion actively recreate
Itself in this way as an experience in another soul?
And the vision then make the error so strong
It can find its way into cosmic development?
(Johannes falls back into his reflections.)
(Maria turns her gaze to Lucifer and hears him speaking.)

LUCIFER:

Here, too, I find the soul's gates open.
I must use the situation and not tarry.
If in this soul, too, – spirit desire is created,
Then the work of love that hints to me
Of danger through Hilary will fail.
I'll be able to destroy Maria's power within him;
Then whatever she's capable of falls to my force.

(Lucifer disappears. At this moment Capesius consciously straightens himself up and in the course of the following words takes on an even surer tone.)

CAPESIUS:

Doubt disappears – I have seen truly; Johannes has
Lived through what I have been permitted to see.
Thus it is also clear his world could only
Open itself to me because that of mine never
Wished to approach that of his *with understanding*.
The spirit's pathway craves for solitude; –

People can only work together
Who face each other with understanding.
Far from the human being, the soul arrives at the
Wide circles of its existence in the worlds of light.
- - - - - - - - - -

Father Felix is shown me as an example;
On pathways foreign to others,
He seeks the spirit light in his proud solitude;
And successful was his seeking – because he always
Held his understanding nature apart from himself.
I'm going to go on striving like him, and your work
Which burdens this clairvoyant force with
Earthly existence will no longer entice Capesius.

(He leaves)

MARIA:

So it is with human beings when our better self
Sinks into spirit sleep, and the Powers of Desire
Nurture our being, until awakening again illumines
With light the real nature of our spirit.
This is the sleep that all of us must sleep
Before the forces of clairvoyance awaken us.
We know nothing of this waking sleep;
We seem awake – because we are *always* sleeping.
The seers sleep, when from their own true existence
They have forced themselves into this waking state.
Capesius will now withdraw himself from us.
Not simply a flighty act of Will draws him back,
His very condition draws him away from our goals.
Not he is bringing about this turning away from us.
One can see the stern signs of the Powers of Destiny.
So now the rest of us will definitely have to devote
Our forces to our work in greater measure.

JOHANNES:

> Maria, do not demand of Johannes
> That at this time he arm for new goals
> This soul which just like that other one °
> Needs spirit sleep so it can cultivate
> Its now germinating forces to maturity.
> I know that one day I will be bold enough
> To work for spirit worlds – but not *now*
> Demand that I be active – not *now*. –
> Consider that I drove Capesius away. – – –
> Were I mature enough for this work – *he'd* be, too.

MARIA:

> Drove Capesius away? – you – you're dreaming.

JOHANNES:

> *Knowing* I dreamed … yes, dreaming, I *awoke*.
> What was but shine before cosmic Powers –
> Has shown itself before me as a sign of my maturity.
> I know quite well my *desiring* was I myself.
> And *only* the thinking was another self.
> Thus Johannes stood before my soul
> As he once was before the spirit laid hold of him
> And filled him with the second self.
> He is not dead, Johannes's – – – life of desires,
> That makes him into the companion of my soul.
> I may, indeed, have stunned him, but not overcome.
> He demands the right to his own existence
> When this self – – – must sink into sleep,
> And *always* awake – – – *that* it's not capable of.
> Thus it also slept at that moment
> When Capesius could experience within himself
> How that other one tore me out of my self.
> My dreaming became a sign for him from destiny.

Thus in me and not in him has worked the force
That drove him away – that forbids us
To direct our spirit towards this earthly work.

MARIA:

The spirit forces are coming – summon them. –
Direct your gaze to the spirit world's foundations
And then wait until those forces in the depths
Sense what in your own self
Behaves in a similar way to their being.
They'll conjure you before your inner eye,
Which will let them and you become a unity.
Banish your senses' disturbing conversation, then
The spirit in you will speak with those spirit beings,
And to this spirit conversation, listen in.
It'll carry you to the spheres of light
And bind you to your spirit individuality. °
What is dawning in you from those lived-out times
Will then appear clearly to you
In the cosmic light and will not compel you
Because you'll be able to give it direction.
Compare it with the beings of the elements,
With the shades and with spectres of all kinds,
Also place it next to some of the demons °
And so experience what it's really worth;
But then fathom *yourself* in the realm of those spirits
That connect Primal Beginning to Primal Beginning,
That know themselves close to cosmic seed forces and
Give direction to the spheres' goal-aimed thoughts.
Such a cosmic vision will strengthen you so that
Within all this spirit fluctuation you may unite the
Existence in your soul kernel as being to yourself.
- - - - - - - - - -
- - - - - - - - - -

The Spirit bids my self make this known to you;
Simply listen now to what you are aware of,
Though not yet wedded to within your soul depths.

JOHANNES *(clearly showing that he has roused himself to a strong decision)*:

I will hear it – will defy my self.

(From both sides come elemental spirits. From the left come gnome-like beings. They have a steel-gray, but in comparison to humans, small figure; they are almost completely head, but this is bent over forward. They have long, mobile limbs awkward for walking, but suited to gestures. From the right come sylph-like, slender, almost headless figures, whose feet and hands are a cross between fins and wings; some of them are blue-green, the others yellow-reddish. With the yellow-reddish ones, the figure is fashioned with sharper contures; with the blue-green ones, more undefined. The words these figures speak are produced with expressive, right up to dance-like, gestures.)

CHORUS OF GNOME SPIRITS:
We're hard'ning, we're strength'ning
The dusty stuff's bright glitter;
We're loos'ning, we're pounding
The hardened crusty sediments;
We nimbly crush the firm
And slowly firm the loose
With spirits of our bodies
Woven out of reasoning's stuff
That fully clever was,
When human souls were dreaming,
While at earth beginnings sleeping.

CHORUS OF SYLPH SPIRITS:

> We're weaving, we're teasing
> What's wove of water and air;
> We're sev'ring, we're scatt'ring
> The enlivened sun seed-forces;
> We're caref'ly thick'ning light's own powers
> We're wisely nixing fruiting forces
> With the bodies of our souls
> Flowing from sensation's rays
> That ever livingly glitter,
> So human beings living
> Enjoy earth-becoming's meaning.

CHORUS OF GNOME SPIRITS:

> We're laughing, we're giggling,
> We're mocking, we're grinning,
> When human senses bumble
> And human minds do stumble
> On seeing our production
> And thinking they're so wisely grasping
> What spirits of our age abiding
> Afore their stupid eyes are conj'ring.

CHORUS OF SYLPH SPIRITS:

> We're caring, we're tending,
> We're rip'ning, we're springing,
> When life adawning human children
> And wrong aweaving human oldies
> Are on our workings gnawing
> And childish or even oldish
> In streaming time are dumb enjoying
> What we're eternally pondering.
> *(These spirit beings move towards the background as if coming*
> *together in two clusters and remain visible there.*

From the left appear the three soul forces Philia, Astrid, Luna with the "Other Philia".)

PHILIA:

They're raying forth brightness
As love-giving light
To the blessedly ripe;
Gently they're warming
And powerfully heating
Where the growing wills
To active existence,
So active existence
Enchants the souls greatly
Who surrender in love
To the raying forth light.

ASTRID:

They're weaving in life
As helpers creating
In sprouting up beings.
The earth they are bursting
And breezes they're thick'ning
That change may be seen
In striving creation.
So striving creation
Makes happy the spirits
That feel themselves weaving
In life's own creating.

LUNA:

They're thoughtfully pressing
As active creators
This shapeable stuff;
The edges they're sharp'ning,

The surfaces flat'ning,
So with meaning are built
The arching out forms,
So the arching out forms
Are enthusing the Wills
To sensible building
As active creators.

THE OTHER PHILIA:

They're plucking the blossoms
As carefree availers
In enchanted endeavors;
They're dreaming the true,
They're guarding delusion,
So sleeping seed kernels
Are awakened to life;
And awakened dreaming
To souls is revealing
The enchanted weaving
Of this their own being.

(These four soul forces and the spirit beings disappear to the right; Johannes, who during the previous events was sunk in deep reflection, rouses himself.)

JOHANNES:

"And awakened dreaming
To souls is revealing
The enchanted weaving
Of this their own being."
These are the words still ringing clearly
Within my soul – what I saw before
Drew away out of my soul in confusion. – –
- - - - - - - - - -

But what force is aroused in me when I think:
The enchanted weaving
Of this their own being – – –
(He again falls back into his reflections; there appears before
him as his own thought form a group composed of: the Spirit of
Johannes's Youth, Lucifer to the left of it, Theodora's soul to the
right.)

THE SPIRIT OF JOHANNES'S YOUTH:
    The existence of your desires nourishes my life,
    My breath laps up the dreams of your youth;
    I am in existence when you don't want to penetrate
    Into those worlds I am not able to find.
    When you lose me in *yourself*, I have to perform
    In pain my wretched service for the horrid shades; –
    O sustainer of my existence – – – do not leave me. –

LUCIFER:
    He won't leave you – in the depth of his being
    I can see passions for light
    That cannot follow Maria's trail. – –
    When these, with the brilliance they produce,
    Fully illuminate Johannes's creating soul,
    He won't be able to squander the fruits
    They must produce in that realm
    Where love wants to reign without beauty.
    Then the self wanting to throw away his best forces
    To the shades through over-estimation of learning
    Will no longer seem so valuable to him.
    When wisdom illuminates his desires,
    Their worth will be gloriously revealed to him;
    He can take them for only little worth as long as
    They still maintain themselves in soul darkness.
    Until they are able to reach the light of wisdom,

I want to loyally care for you – by means of
That light I can find in human soul foundations.
- - - - - - - - - -

He is still lacking in pity for your sorrows,
He always leaves you to sink into the realm of
Spectres when he strives for his heights of light.
Then he can forget that you, his child,
Must lead a painful, enchanted existence.
In future, however, you'll have me at your side
When as a shade you freeze because of his guilt.
With that right that Lucifer preserves
(*With the word "Lucifer" the Spirit of Johannes's Youth winces.*)
For himself from the laws of ancient worlds,
I'll secure for myself in the depths of his soul
What he leaves unguarded in his spirit's flight.
Then I'll bring you the treasure that will relieve
Your dark solitude in the realm of the shades.
Yet you'll only be fully freed of enchantment
When he can *unite* himself with you again.
He can put that off – – *not* prevent it.
For Lucifer will protect his rights.

THEODORA:

O Spirit Child, you must live out Johannes's youth
In the dark realm of the shades. – From light-filled,
Love-warmed realms, the soul that protects
Johannes lovingly inclines herself to you.
She wishes to free you from these enchanted circles
If you wish to take from her the feelings that
Will bring about an existence in blessedness for you.
I wish to unite you with the elements
That unconsciously work in cosmic expanses,
Ever withdrawing themselves from soul wakefulness.

With the Earth Spirits you'll be able to fashion forms
And with the Fire Souls ray forth forces if you
Offer up your existence as knower to that Will
Whose light strengthens without human wisdom.
You wish to preserve your learning, which is only
Half your own, from Lucifer and perform
Services of value for Johannes.
I shall take out of his soul existence
What will make him need your existence
And hand him refreshing spirit sleep.

LUCIFER:

She'll never be able to give you beauty,
Because I boldly intend to take it from her.

THEODORA:

From noble feelings I wish to germinate beauty –
And let it ripen in the service of sacrifice.

LUCIFER:

She'll tear your free will from you
And give it to the spirits that rule in darkness.

THEODORA:

I shall awaken that spirit-filled vision
That even knows itself free of Lucifer.
(*Lucifer, Theodora and the Spirit of Johannes's Youth disappear.
Johannes, awakening out of his reflections, sees the "Other Philia"
coming towards him.*)

THE OTHER PHILIA:

And awakened dreaming
To souls is revealing
The enchanted weaving
Of this their own being.

JOHANNES:

> O enigmatic spirit – through your words
> I entered this world! – – Of its wonders
> Only this One is – – important to my soul:
> Whether the shade wanting to reveal itself to me
> With Theodora and Lucifer abides
> As a living being in the realm of the spirit?

THE OTHER PHILIA:

> It *lives* – it is awakened to existence through you.
> Just as everything shows itself image-like
> In a mirror that lets light ray onto its surface,
> So what you behold in the realm of the spirit
> Before full maturity gives you the right
> To such vision – livingly reflects itself
> In the realm of half-awakened shadow spirits.

JOHANNES:

> It's only an *image* that is thus reflected through me?

THE OTHER PHILIA:

> But an image that *lives* and maintains itself in life
> As long as you still preserve a lived-out existence
> Within you, which you can certainly stun,
> But at present, in truth, not yet overcome. –
> Johannes, your awakeness remains a delusion
> Until you yourself release the shade
> For which your *guilt* creates an enchanted life.

JOHANNES:

> How can I thank this spirit who brings
> True advice into my soul – – I *must follow it.*

(The curtain falls slowly while the "Other Philia" and Johannes remain standing with relaxed gestures.)

SCENE THREE

The landscape scenery as in the second scene.
Magnus Bellicosus, Romanus, Torquatus and Hilary come from
the right side in such a way that the following, which they speak
while standing still, may be thought of as the continuation of a
conversation they have been having during their walk. Those taking
part have come to a standstill just because the conversation has
taken on such great importance for them.

BELLICOSUS:
> And if that rigid mind won't bend,
> How is the work Hilary wants to lovingly
> Dedicate to human service to make progress!

ROMANUS:
> What our friend's loyal co-worker
> Has brought forward as grounds for objection
> Doesn't carry weight just with those people
> Who form their own opinions for themselves,
> Keeping in mind life's external demands – isn't it
> Also in harmony with the true opinion of the Mystics?

BELLICOSUS:
> For all that, it's not found in the spiritual circle
> That does firmly embrace our goals.
> Benedictus's pupils have succeeded us
> In our work as Mystics – and now Hilary wants
> To create a site for their activity
> Which is to allow their spiritual fruits to mature.
> The wise Powers of Destiny have united them
> With us in the Temple, and our friend here
> Is simply giving answer to the directions revealed
> In the Temple as the call of spiritual obligation.

ROMANUS:

>Are you also certain you correctly understand
>This spiritual call? For it's far more likely
>Benedictus himself as well as the pupils
>He has led to the spirit after his own manner
>Should still keep themselves in the inner Temple
>And not yet enter on that rough road
>Down which Hilary wants to lead them. –
>Spiritual vision, even for him, is all too easily
>Transformed into a dreamy soul sleep.

BELLICOSUS:

>These words I hadn't thought to hear from you.
>They might well be allowed for that co-worker
>Of Hilary who can only get hold of
>A knowledge of limited worth from books,
>But its incumbent on you to recognize the signs
>Being displayed on the mystic path.
>The manner in which Benedictus's pupils
>Were led to us speaks clearly to our souls.
>They have been united with us so we may follow
>What is being revealed to their clairvoyance.

TORQUATUS:

>For all that, another sign reveals that
>The copious blessings of the spirit Powers
>Have not flowed to the work
>Put before our souls in the Temple.
>Capesius has separated himself from Benedictus
>And the circle of his pupils.
>That he hasn't yet experienced in himself
>The full soul wakefulness Benedictus is already
>Looking for in him, simply throws murky shadows
>On the teacher's own certainty as well.

BELLICOSUS:

    The gifts of the seer still lie far off for me,
    Yet I have often felt how certain happenings
    Release an intuitive knowing in my soul.
    When for the first time I saw Capesius
    In our circle at our place of consecration,
    The thought haunted me that destiny had placed him
    At the same time both near and far from us.

ROMANUS:

    I can appreciate this intuition of yours,
    But at the same moment, *I* was intuiting
    None of these new friends of the Mystics
    Is so closely united with me
    Through the Powers of Destiny as is Strader.
    For *me*, such an intuition is quite simply a sign
    Pointing my soul in the direction
    In which I may intelligently seek,
    And when I then turn to deeds, I first of all
    Wipe out the intuition energizing my thinking. –
    This is what the strict rules of mysticism teach *me*.
    I certainly feel myself closely connected
    In the spirit domain with Benedictus's pupils,
    Nonetheless, if from this inner circle of Mystics
    I'm supposed to seek the way back to earthly life,
    Then I would venture it only at Strader's side.
    (Ahriman appears at the right in the mountain landscape
    background and disappears to the left without being noticed.)

TORQUATUS:

    Hilary's loyal co-worker simply
    Doesn't recognize in Strader that sure spirit
    That can effectively further outer life,
    And when I myself allow my inner voice to speak

Then it reveals to me he totally lacks
The right soul-mood for mysticism.
What outer signs are able to convince him of,
What his understanding grasps of spirit existence,
This arouses his strong impulse for research; yet
From inner spiritual experience he still stands far.
What could this man's spiritual creations be
Other than a dark, mystical web of dreams?

ROMANUS:

Until now he has not advanced far enough
Along the spirit pathway of his friends to come
Into contact with those opponents of the soul
Which are so dangerous for some Mystics
When they follow them into sense existence.

BELLICOSUS:

If you believe him free from such opponents,
Really nothing hinders you from working for him
So that this great work Hilary wants
To carry out through him may succeed.
When our friend's co-worker hears
How you revere the man whom he fails to have
Even a little respect for, his judgement
Will certainly be shaken. You alone
May be capable of winning him for the matter.
It's known to him you've always had success
In outer life in everything you've ever done,
After judiciously thinking things out beforehand.

ROMANUS:

My dear Hilary, if you would place Strader
At your side and without delusion
Would hold distant from your work

438

Those other spirit pupils of Benedictus,
Then you'd *not* be alone – then I'd offer you
Not only what Bellicosus has just now demanded
As my help, I'd also want to actively serve
This splendid plan of Strader's
With everything I possess in outer goods.

HILARY:

How could you imagine Strader would now
Separate himself from Benedictus's pupils –
And without them simply follow his own spirit goals.
The others stand as *close* to him as he to himself.

ROMANUS:

That they are humanly close to him may be right;
To also imagine himself spiritually united with them
Only *that* part in his soul could do
Which is still being held deep in *spirit-sleep;*
But it seems to me that how *that part* can ripen
To awakened life must come to light very soon.
(The four exit towards the left side.)
*(Coming from the right side, Capesius, Strader, Felix Bald and
Mrs. Bald; as if come to a standstill in their conversation because
the following content is so important to them.)*

CAPESIUS:

Simply to follow the spirit on inner soul paths,
This alone can I do at present. If I were to burden
Myself with this outer work in order to bring
The spirit to existence within the senses' realm –
I'd have to presume to grasp
The ground of existence in worlds whose nature,
Until now, has not yet become reality within me.
Of cosmic existence, I can only behold

As much of it as has been fashioned within *me*.
How am I to create what is of use to the others
If in that creating I am only enjoying my self?

STRADER:

If I understand you, you mean only the imprint
Of your own nature would be given to all
Your creating and thus, in this work, convey
Only your own existence to the outer world?

CAPESIUS:

That's how it is until I can encounter
A foreign being with my own inner world.
How far I can already penetrate into another being
I had to painfully admit to myself
When for a short moment I was awakened to clarity.

FELIX BALD:

You are saying something I've never heard from you. —
Yet never was I able — — to understand you so well
As now, since nothing but your self is speaking.
In your speech sounds forth the mood of the mysticism
I have sought with discipline through many years
And that alone is able to perceive the light within
Which, through bright vision, the human spirit can
Knowingly experience itself in the cosmic spirit.

CAPESIUS:

Because I intuited how close to you I've come,
I've fled to you from an impulse
That would have deadened my inner world.

STRADER:

Oft I found understandable – what you're now saying;

I held it for wisdom then – – yet not a word
Of your discourse is understandable to me *now*.
Capesius and father Felix, *both* ...
Hiding dim meanings in transparent words ...
- - - - - - - - - -

Am I not experiencing how your words are simply
The outer cloak of forces – – of soul forces,
Banishing me from you into worlds
Lying very far from your type of spirit?
Worlds I don't wish to seek for – because
I must love those of *yours* in my deepest soul.
I could easily bear the opposition
Now threatening my work from without.
Yes, even if all my acts of Will
Now shattered on this opposition –
I'd be able to maintain myself;
But your worlds I cannot do without.

FELIX BALD:

Human beings cannot find the spirit world
If they want to unlock it through *seeking*.
I was once made very happy by you
When you spoke before me about your mechanism –
When what you did not want to achieve for yourself
Through intellectual seeking gave you illumination.
Then you were near to the true mystic mood.
- - - - - - - - - -

Striving for *nothing* – simply being peacefully still,
The inner state of soul totally expectation – –
This is the mystic mood. – Whoever *awakens* it
Leads their inner nature to the realm of light.
Outer work will not allow of such a mood.
If you wish to seek for *that* through mysticism,
You'll deaden life with mystical delusions.

STRADER:

I have need of you – – but I don't find you. –
This existence uniting us – – you don't value it.
How can people find each other for cosmic work
If the Mystics never leave their own existence?

FELIX BALD:

You cannot bear the delicate existence of vision
Into the world you *actively* give yourself to
Without that existence dissolving for you
As that world receives you at its boundary.
In devoutness, revering spirit Rulers,
Letting spirit vision repose within the heart – –
Thus do the Mystics approach the world of *deeds*.

CAPESIUS:

And if they want to enter it *otherwise*,
Then it will indeed show them the effects of error
But not the bright individuality of wisdom.
I was able to look into one person's soul. –
I knew my vision wasn't deceiving me,
Yet I saw only the error of that soul.
For me it was *that*, just because I had spoiled
My spirit vision through desire for outer deeds.

STRADER:

So speaks Capeseus who has advanced
Far ahead of me along soul paths; – –
And yet *for me*, spirit vision only arises if my soul
May devote itself to thoughts of doing and thus find
Itself living in the hope it can build sites for
The spirit where it will want to ignite that light
That rays warmingly through the spirit worlds and
That seeks its new home within earth existence

Through the sense activity of a human being.

- - - - - - - - - -

Am I the son of error – – not your son,
You wide, wisdom-filled worlds of the spirit!
(As if only for a moment, Strader turns away from his
companions; he now has the following spirit vision – Benedictus,
Maria, Ahriman appear – though only as his thought forms, yet
in real spiritual communion; at first Benedictus with Ahriman,
then Maria.)

BENEDICTUS:

In the wide, wisdom-filled worlds of the spirit
You intuit help for the pain that question brings,
Pain that makes the ultimate secret of your soul life
Into a burden for your earthly thinking.
The answer you shall hear from your soul depths
In the manner the spirit expanses
Wish to reveal it to you through my voice;
But learn to understand what you imagine knowing,
What you very often venture to speak out
And yet only dream within your own soul existence.
Give to your dream the life I have been enjoined
(Ahriman appears.)
To reach out to you from the spirit,
But transform into that dream existence what you
Can draw for yourself from the senses by thinking.
Capesius and father Felix are banishing you
From the spirit light they are beholding.
They are laying an abyss between themselves and you.
Do not complain that they've prepared this for you,
Instead look into your abyss.

AHRIMAN:

Sure, do it!

You'll behold what of the human spirit seems of worth
To you in the broad sweep of cosmic evolution. It
Might be good for you if other spirits were to show
It to you while you were in a dulled-down soul sleep,
But Benedictus'll show it to you while you're awake,
So you'll kill the answer for yourself while seeing.
Yah sure, do it.

STRADER:

I shall do it. But how? –
Confused figures? They're changing – they're tearing –
The one is tearing at the other – a battle – –
The spectres are furiously attacking one another –
Destruction reigns, begetting darkness: –
From the darkness now other shadow beings.
Around them etheric brightness – weaving reddishly;
Quite distinctly, one of the figures frees itself;
It's coming towards me – the abyss is sending it to me.
(*Maria comes forth out of the abyss.*)

MARIA:

You're beholding demons – build up your strength,
They're not like this – they're appearing before you
As what they're not. When you can maintain them
Until they can make their spectral beings shine
Before your soul existence, they'll have for you
The worth they can have in cosmic development;
But the vision fades away for you even before
They've unfolded the strength to appear.
Irradiate them with your own light.
Where is your light? – You're raying out darkness. –
Recognize your darkness – all around you – you're
Conveying your confusing darkness into the light.
You experience it when you create it through yourself,

But then you never experience your creating.
You wish to forget your craving to create.
Unknown to you, it rules within your own being
Because you're too cowardly to ray out your own light.
You wish to enjoy this light of yours.
You only want to enjoy your self in it.
You are seeking yourself – and seek in forgetfulness.
You let your dreaming self sink into yourself.

AHRIMAN:

Yah, listen to her – she can solve your problems,
But you'll find her solution – not your own.
She gives you wisdom – so that you can direct
Your steps with her towards foolishness.
She might be good for you – at another time,
When the bright spirit-day'll appear to you;
But when Maria speaks like this within your dreams,
She kills the solution for you while advising.
Yah, listen to her.

STRADER:

What do these words want to say?
Maria, are they born out of the light?
Out of my light? – Is it my darkness
Out of which they sound forth? Benedictus, speak.
Who is climbing out of the abyss giving me advice?

BENEDICTUS:

She has sought you out at your own abyss.
Thus do spirits seek out individuals in order to protect
Them from the beings that fashion spectres for souls
And then so confuse the rule of the Cosmic Spirit
With the darkness that the souls can only really know
Themselves within the net of their own existence.
Look still further into your abyss.

STRADER:

What is coming to life now in the depths of my abyss?

BENEDICTUS:

Behold the shades, to the right those bluish-red,
They are tempting Felix – and see the others –
On the left – red brightening softly into yellow,
They are pressing in towards Capesius.
Both feel the power of those shades; – –
In solitude both are creating for themselves the
Light that lames the shades that deceive human souls.

AHRIMAN:

He'd do better if he'd show you your shades –
But he's hardly capable of that; –
It isn't really that he lacks good will.
He simply doesn't notice where to look for them.
They're standing right behind you, disturbingly close –
Indeed, you yourself are covering those nearest him.

STRADER:

So here at my abyss I now hear words
I considered a foolish utterance
When Hilary's adviser spoke them to me! – – –

MARIA:

Father Felix is hardening the weapons he needs
To wipe out his danger – another sort is needed
By whoever has to travel your soul paths;
What Capesius is fashioning as sword for himself
To bravely join in battle with his soul's opponents
Would change into a shadow sword for Strader
Were he to commence with it the spirit battle
The Powers of Destiny have preordained for souls

Who must energetically recreate within earthly
Activities a spirit being which is ripe for deeds.
You cannot use their weapons for yourself,
Yet you must recognize them so you can judiciously
Forge your own for yourself from this soul material.
*(The figures of Benedictus, Ahriman, and Maria disappear; that
is, as seen externally, Strader returns from his spirit vision; he
looks around for Capesius, Felix Bald and Mrs. Bald; these come
towards him again; he has seated himself on a rocky outcrop.)*

FELIX BALD:

My dear Strader, didn't the spirit just now
Carry you far away from us? – It seemed so to me.
*(He pauses, waiting so Strader can say something, but since he
remains silent, he continues on.)*
I didn't want to heartlessly drive you
Out of our circle down some other avenue of life.
I only wanted to prevent you from giving yourself up
Still more to the delusion confusing you.
What a spirit beholds in spirit should only
Be spiritually received and experienced by the soul.
How foolish it would be if Felicia wanted to take
Those fairy tale beings she is alive to in her soul,
And that also only want to be experienced in a soul,
And let them dance upon a puppet stage.
Then all the enchantment would be gone.

MRS. BALD:

I really have been silent long enough.
But I speak now, when you even want to make
The fairy sprites happy with your mystic mood.
They'd really be thankful if their strength were
First sucked out of them by you, and then

They were newly suckled back to life with mysticism.
All due respect to mysticism —
But for me it simply remains
Far from my fairy tale realms.

CAPESIUS:

Felicia, wasn't it your fairy tales
That first showed me the spirit pathway?
What you so often called up before
My thirsting soul as air and water sprites
Were messengers to me from that world
Into which I now mystically seek entrance.

MRS. BALD:

Yet ever since you've come to our house
With these new mystic ways, you've asked
But little what my beautiful magical beings want.
You still often let the ones pass
That wear a dignified and serious expression,
But the ones wildly dancing full of joy
You find quite mystically uncomfortable.

CAPESIUS:

I don't doubt, Felicia, that sometime later
The deep meaning of even those magical beings
That wish to reveal earnestness in a merry mask
Will be unlocked for me,
But my strength does not yet reach that far.

FELIX BALD:

Felicia, you know how I love them,
The fairy folk that disclose themselves to you,
But to imagine them embodied
In mechanical puppets — it's repulsive.

MRS. BALD:

> I haven't yet so presented them before you;
> For that, *you* stand – too high; but I was glad
> When I learned of Strader's plan
> And heard also Thomasius was endeavoring
> To render the spirit sensible in matter.
> In spirit, I saw my fairy princes
> And my fire souls, artistically beautiful,
> Dancing joyfully in a thousand puppet plays.
> So already I've let them, supremely happy
> In the thought, eagerly find their way
> Into the children's playrooms. °

(*Curtain*)

SCENE FOUR

The mountain landscape of the second and third scenes. The Office
Manager and Romanus speak the following during a pause in their
walk. Later: Johannes, the Double of Johannes Thomasius; the
Spirit of Johannes's Youth; the Guardian of the Threshold; Ahriman;
Benedictus, Maria, Strader, The Soul of Theodora.

OFFICE MANAGER:

>You know those mystic friends of Hilary,
>And in you I can recognize a judicious man who
>Ever keeps watch on his power of sound judgement,
>Whether demanded in daily work or by the mystic arts;
>That's why I value the opinion that you harbor.
>Yet *how* am I to understand what you've just said? – –
>It seems right to you that Strader's friends should
>Still hold themselves back in the spirit domain
>And not at present direct their clairvoyant forces
>To creating for the senses. Wouldn't the same pathway
>Show itself to be equally dangerous for Strader?
>To me, his spiritual approach seems to demonstrate
>Nature Demons always blind him
>When with his strong desire – he seeks the way
>To his deeds within an outer social project. – –
>The judicious mystic knows one first has to
>Properly create the forces within oneself in order
>To be able to offer resistance to these opponents;
>But on Strader's spirit pathway, it seems the sight
>For such opponents has not yet matured for him.

ROMANUS:

>Yet the good spirits guiding individuals
>Who still stand quite outside the spirit
>Have not yet forsaken him.

When such spirits make alliance with other beings
That are of service to *their* spirit mood,
Then these spirits turn away from the Mystics. °
In Strader's approach, I can quite clearly feel
How Nature Demons still give freely to his self
The fruits of their *good* forces.

OFFICE MANAGER:

And nothing other than simply these feelings
Impel you to presume good spirits in Strader?
You offer little and demand a lot.

- - - - - - - - - -

In future I'm supposed to consult these spirits
When I want to undertake activities at this place
Where for so long I've been permitted to serve
The meaning of work and that true spirit °
With which the father of Hilary was bound up –
And which I can still hear from his grave – –
Even if the son doesn't have an ear for it!
What would the spirit of that virtuous man say
If it now looked upon those confused spirits
The son is striving to bring into the firm?
I know it, that spirit, that maintained itself
In that body for ninety years; it taught me
The genuine mysteries of work in those times
When *it* was still involved in this concern,
While the son crept off to the Mystics' Temple.

ROMANUS:

My friend, is it then unknown to you about me
How highly I esteem that spirit?
That old man, whom you have quite rightly chosen
As example for yourself, certainly served it.
And to serve *it* I have striven as well

From my childhood until the present day;
But I, too, crept off to the Mystics' Temple.
I faithfully planted in my soul depths
What they were willing to bestow on me;
Yet my understanding left the mood of the Temple
At the door when it entered back into life.
I knew that *in this way* I would best bear
The force of that mood into my earthly life;
I did, *however*, bring my *soul* out of the Temple
Back into this activity. – For *it* is good,
If earthly understanding does not disturb it.

OFFICE MANAGER:

And do you find Strader's spiritual approach
Looks even remotely similar to yours?
At your side I always knew I was free
From the spirit beings Strader brings me.
I certainly feel, even when he speaks confusedly,
How through his words and his being the spirits
Of the elements pour themselves out livingly,
Actively, revealing what the senses cannot grasp;
But just this pushes me away from him.

ROMANUS

Your words, my friend, strike deep into my heart.
Ever since I drew near to Stader, I've come
To perceive how the thoughts I've experienced
From him are endowed with a quite special force.
They penetrate into me just like my own;
And one day I said to myself, what if you owe,
Not to *yourself*, what if your soul owes to *him*
The force that enabled you to mature into a man!
And this feeling was soon followed by a second one:
What if, in regard to everything that makes me useful

In social projects and of service to humanity, what
If I were in debt from an earlier earthly existence?

OFFICE MANAGER:

That's just what I've had to experience with him. –
When one draws near him, the spirit working
Through him then powerfully draws ones soul in.
If your strong soul could succumb to him,
How then should I protect that of mine
Were I to unite with him in work?

ROMANUS:

It must be left up to you alone to find out
How you should properly relate to him.
I believe Strader's power will not harm *me*
Since I have formed thoughts for myself
About how he may have achieved that power.

OFFICE MANAGER:

Achieved – he himself – – power – and over you –
The dreamer – over *you*, social life's master artist!

ROMANUS:

If I may be so venturous as to suggest it,
In Strader might now live a spirit
Who in an earlier earthly life may have brought
Itself to extraordinary heights of soul, – – –
May have known much that other people of his time
Could not even have had an inkling of; – –
It might have been possible that at some point
Thoughts took their origin from his spirit
And then were able to find their way into
The general social life of earthly human beings,
Thoughts by means of which people of my type

Have now drawn capabilities into themselves. –
What for thoughts I made into my own
From my environment in my youth, might,
In fact, have originated from this spirit.

OFFICE MANAGER:

And does it also then seem permissable to you
To attribute thoughts, which are clearly valuable
As life teachings, to Strader in particular?

ROMANUS:

I'd be a dreamer if I took up what you're pointing at.
I don't spin a dream-web of social teachings
With eyes tight shut. Simply to doze on in thoughts
That cacoon themselves was never my approach to life. –
I look on Strader with open eyes.
How this man establishes himself as an individual
With everything belonging to him, and *how* he acts;
Even what is unproductive in him; – and it becomes
Clear I had to form my judgement about his gifts
Just as I have now stated it.
As if this man had already stood before my eyes
Many hundred years ago, that's how I now
Experience him before me in spirit;
And that I am awake – I know *full well*.
I shall remain by Hilary's side;
What must happen, will happen.
Think over his social plans a bit more deeply.

OFFICE MANAGER:

For me it's now truly of greater import
To think over what you yourself have confided to me.
*(The Office Manager and Romanus walk on further into the
landscape. Sunk in thought, Johannes comes from another*

direction and sits down on a rocky outcrop. At first Johannes
alone, then his Double, the Spirit of Johannes's Youth, at the end
the Guardian of the Threshold.)

JOHANNES *(alone)*

How astonished I was when Capesius disclosed
That the inner existence of my soul
Was revealed in his spirit vision.
What had already been clearly shown me
Many years ago could thus become obscured. – –
That everything living within human souls
Works on in the spirit's outer realms,
I already knew long ago – I could *forget* it. –
When Benedictus showed me the pathways
To my first clairvoyance – at that time
I could clearly behold in pictures through the spirit
Capesius and Strader at other ages of their lives.
I saw how the strongly made forms of their thinking
Brought about rippling circles in cosmic existence.
I know all this quite *well* – and knew it not
When I beheld it through Capesius.
The existence in me that knows was asleep.
How I was closely bound up with Capesius
In a long past earthly life,
Even this I knew a long time ago, – –
Yet at that moment I knew it not.
How can I keep a watch on what I know?
(A voice out of the distance, that of Johannes's Double.)

The enchanted weaving
Of this their own being.

JOHANNES:

And awakened dreaming

To souls is revealing
The enchanted weaving
Of this their own being.
(*While Johannes is speaking this sentence, his Double comes up to him. Johannes does not recognize it but believes "The Other Philia" is approaching."*)

JOHANNES:

You are here once again, enigmatic spirit,
You who brought true counsel to my soul.

THE DOUBLE:

Johannes, your awakening remains a delusion
Until you *yourself* set free that shade
For whom your *guilt* creates a spellbound life.

JOHANNES:

For the second time you speak these words.
I *want* to follow them. – Show me the way.

THE DOUBLE:

Johannes, let live in the realm of the shades
What is lost within your self,
But give it light from your spirit light
So it will not have to suffer pain.

JOHANNES:

That shade I have indeed stunned,
But not yet overcome; thus it will have to remain
A spellbound shadow being among shades
Until I can again *unite* myself with it.

THE DOUBLE:

So now give *me* what you owe that being;

The force of love driving you to it,
The hope of your heart begotten from it,
The fresh new life hidden within it,
The fruits of long past earthly lives
Now lost to you along with its existence,
Oh, give them to me; I'll faithfully bring them to *it*.

JOHANNES:
You know the way to it? – oh, show me.

THE DOUBLE:
I could once penetrate to it in the realm of the shades
Whenever you raised yourself into spirit spheres,
But ever since the Powers of Desire have lured you
And you have turned your mind towards this being,
My strength always fades away when I attempt it;
But if you wish to follow my counsel,
Then that strength could be created anew.

JOHANNES:
I have promised to follow you. –
With the whole strength of my soul,
Oh enigmatic spirit, I will promise it anew;
But if you are able to find the way to it like this,
Then *show* it to me now at this destiny-laden moment.

THE DOUBLE:
I am experiencing it now, but I cannot guide you;
I can only show to your eye of soul
The being that your longing seeks.
(The Spirit of Johannes's Youth appears.)

THE SPIRIT OF JOHANNES'S YOUTH:
I want to be united forever with this spirit

That has been permitted to open your eye of soul,
So that in future you can find me through your vision
When, according to spirit laws, I show myself to you;
Yet you must know this spirit in its reality
At whose side you are now looking on me.
(The Spirit of Johannes's Youth disappears, for Johannes, only now is his Double recognizable.)

JOHANNES:

Not that enigmatic spirit – my other self?

THE DOUBLE:

Now follow me – you promised me –
I now must lead you to the one who rules me.
(The Guardian of the Threshold appears and places himself beside the Double.)

THE GUARDIAN:

Johannes, if you wish to tear this spirit shade
Out of its spellbound world within your soul,
Then deaden the desires leading you astray.
The trail down which you're seeking disappears
As long as you wish to follow it with desires,
For it leads you on along past my Threshold.
Obedient to the willpower of higher beings,
I must here confuse the soul's visions
If desires are living within its spirit sight,
Which must always encounter me here before it is
Permitted to penetrate to the pure light of truth.
(Ahriman enters.)
I hold your self firmly in your line of sight
As long as you approach me with desires.
Even me you only behold as a delusory image
If desire's delusion has bound itself to your vision,

And spirit peacefulness, as a soul body,
Has not yet taken hold in your being.
Intensify those words of strength that you know
So their spirit power overcomes this delusion,
Then recognize me *without your desire,*
And you will see the true form of my being.
I will no longer have to divert your sight,
And you will be free
To turn it towards the spirit domain.

JOHANNES:

Even *you* disclose yourself only to my delusion? ...
Even *you* ... whom I still must truly see
Before I see other beings in the Spiritland.
How am I to know the truth when with each
Further step I find but this one truth:
That I am fashioning my delusion ever thicker.

AHRIMAN:

Don't just let yourself be completely confused by him.
Sure, he does faithfully guard the Threshold,
Even if he's now wearing clothes
You yourself patched together in your mind
From those old horror scenes of yours.
As artist, you really shouldn't have
Fashioned him in that dreadful dramatic style;
In time no doubt, you'll surely do it better.
But even this caricature still can serve your soul.
Not all too much forceful pressing
Is needed to show you what it still is now.
You should have noticed how the Guardian speaks:
Elegiac is his tone, too much of pathos. –
Don't allow him this, and then he'll show you
From whom today he borrows a little to excess.

JOHANNES:

Even the *content* of his *words* were able to deceive?

THE DOUBLE:

Don't ask that of Ahriman, who simply must
Always feel delight at every contradiction.

JOHANNES

Who am I to ask?

THE DOUBLE:

Simply ask your self.
I want to properly arm you with my force so that,
Awakened, you may find the standpoint in yourself
That may look out from where no desire burns in you.
Strengthen yourself.

JOHANNES:

The enchanted weaving
Of this their own being.
Enchanted weaving of this my own being,
Inform me of where no desire is burning in me.

*(The Guardian disappears; in his place appear Benedictus and
Maria. Ahriman disappears.)*

MARIA:

Even me you only see as a delusory image because
Desire's delusion is united with your vision.

BENEDICTUS:

And spirit peacefulness, as a soul body,
Has not yet taken hold in your being.
(The Double, Benedictus, and Maria disappear.)

JOHANNES (*alone*):

    Bendictus, Maria, they – the Guardian!

    How can they appear to me as Guardian?

    - - - - - - - - - -

    Though I've been with you many long years – –

    The enchanted weaving of this my own being

    Now strictly orders me to seek you. –

    (*He exits towards the left side of the mountain scenery.*)

    (*Strader, Benedictus, and Maria come from the right side of the mountain scenery.*)

STRADER:

    In spiritual communion with you both

    At the deep abyss of my own being,

    You gave my soul vision those wise hints

    That, though not understandable at this time,

    Will work on within my soul existence

    And certainly solve those riddles of my life

    That are hindering my striving.

    I feel within me that force your activities

    Give to pupils on the spirit pathway,

    Thus I shall be quite capable of performing

    The services you'll need for the work

    Hilary wants to dedicate to humanity.

    Capesius, its true, we'll have to do without. –

    Energetic activity by the others will never wholly

    Be able to replace the part he plays in this,

    Yet what should happen, will happen

BENEDICTUS:

    What should happen, will happen.

    These words express the stage of your maturity,

    Yet they find no echo in the soul existence

    Of our other spirit friends.

Thomasius is not yet armed to bear
This spirit force into sense existence.
Thus he also wishes to draw back from our work.
Through him, a sign of destiny is shown us;
Now all of us must seek still other possibilities.

STRADER:

And isn't Maria, *aren't you* going to be there then? °

BENEDICTUS:

Maria must take Johannes with her
If she is to find the path of truth back
From spirit existence into the realm of the senses.
So wills that solemn Guardian now
Who strictly guards the border of both realms.
She cannot yet stand at your side.
For you, this should be taken as a sure sign
That at this time you cannot really yet
Find your way into the domain of matter.

STRADER:

So then I must remain alone with my goals!
Oh solitude, was it *you* that sought me out
As I stood at Felix Bald's side?

BENEDICTUS:

What has here been revealed in our circle
Has now taught me to read in the spirit light
Words from the course of your destiny
Previously always withheld from me.
I could see you united with those types of being
Which would work evil if already at this time
They were to intrud their creating
Into what human beings now control;
Yet they do live a seed-like existence within souls

462

In order to be ripen for the earth in the future.
In your soul I saw seeds of such a type;
That you don't recognize them is for your own good.
Through you, they'll first recognize themselves.
For now though, the path is still closed
Leading them over into the domain of matter.

STRADER:

Whatever else besides your words mean to say,
They show me that solitude is seeking me.
It will really have to forge my sword. –
Maria told me this at my abyss.
(Benedictus and Maria draw back; Strader remains alone, the soul of Theodora appears.)

THEODORA'S SOUL:

And in the worlds of light, Theodora will
Engender warmth for you so your spirit sword
Can forcefully smite your soul's opponents.
(She disappears. Strader goes out. Benedictus and Maria come into the foreground alone.)

MARIA:

My wise teacher, never yet have I heard you speak
About their destiny in words of this sort
To pupils who stood at Strader's stage.
Is the course his soul will take to happen so quickly
The force in these words will be beneficial for him?

BENEDICTUS:

Destiny has shown it to me, so it has happened.

MARIA:

And if this force doesn't prove beneficial,

Will the evil effects not smite you, too?

BENEDICTUS:

It won't be evil; yet I don't know
How it will manifest itself in him.
Even though my vision penetrates right now
Into realms where such counsel shines into my soul,
The picture of its effects I cannot yet see.
When I attempt this, the sight dies in the beholding.

MARIA:

Your sight dies in the beholding? – For you, my guide?
Who deadens your sure clairvoyant sight?

BENEDICTUS:

Johannes flees with it into cosmic distances;
We must follow – I hear him calling.

MARIA:

He calls – – his call sounds forth from spirit widths;
Within these sounds rays out a distant fear.

BENEDICTUS:

Thus sounds forth from eternal, empty fields of ice
The call of a mystic friend into cosmic distances.

MARIA:

The coldness of the ice *burns* within my self.
It kindles flames in my soul depths;
The flames are consuming my thinking.

BENEDICTUS:

Within your soul depths is flaming up the fire
Johannes is kindling for himself in the cosmic frost.

MARIA:

The flames are fleeing – – they flee with my thinking;
- - - - - - - - - -
And there on the distant cosmic shoreline of the soul
A raging battle – my own thinking is fighting –
By the stream of nothingness – with cold spirit light. –
My thinking wavers – cold light – it strikes
Hot darkness out of my thinking. – –
What is now rising out of that dark heat? – –
In red flames storms out my self – into the light –
Into the cold light – – of the cosmic fields of ice. –

(*Curtain.*)

SCENE FIVE

The spirit domain. A scene appearing in meaningful streams of color; reddish deepening into fiery red towards the top, blue merging into a dark blue and violet towards the bottom. In the color scheme, the figures entering form a complete whole. *Right:* the Gnome group from the second scene; in front of them, Hilary; at the very front, the Soul Forces; behind Hilary, somewhat raised up, Ahriman. *Left:* raised up, Lucifer; in the foreground, the Soul of Felix Bald. The Souls of Strader and Capesius, Benedictus, Maria, Felicia Bald, the Guardian of the Threshold.

THE SOUL OF FELIX BALD (*standing extreme left, the figure of a penitent, although the robe is light violet with a gold waist cord*):
    Have thanks, O Spirit who wisely directs these worlds,
    My liberator from dark solitudes;
    Your word awakens to life and to work.
    I shall make use of what you give these worlds,
    Worlds I may then ponder on when you let
    That of mine sink into a state of dimness.
    What from my fashionings can create forces for me,
    You'll then bear forth on your rays to these worlds.

LUCIFER (*a bluish-green shining underrobe; a bright shining reddish outer garment in the form of a mantel that extends in wing-like shapes; instead of an aura above, a mitre-like dark-red head-covering set with wings; a blue sword-like shape on the right wing; a yellow planetary sphere-like shape as if carried by the left wing. Lucifer stands somewhat towards the rear and left, raised above the Soul of Felix Bald*):
    My servant, activities of your type have need of
    This Sun Period upon which we now have entered.
    The Earth Star is at present receiving a dimmed light;

This is the period when souls of your type
May best work upon themselves. From
The well-spring of my light, I am letting brightly
Ray out to you the seed impulses for a sense of self.
Gather them in to the strong force of your I.
Within earthly existence they'll blossom forth.
There your soul will seek those blossoms;
It will delight in its own being when it
Can passionately ponder on what it longs for.

THE SOUL OF FELIX BALD *(with its gaze turned towards the group of Gnomes)*:

There in the distance, an illumining existence
Is fading away; in a hazy cloud of images it is floating
Towards the depths; with its floating,
It wishes to give itself weight.

THE SOUL OF HILARY *(in a form similar to a human being, but modified from that of the steel-bluegray Elemental Sprits; head less bowed, limbs similar to a human being)*:

That hazy cloud of desires is the reflection
Of the Earth Star thrown up in the spirit domain,
That Star for which in *this* world you are working up
A thinking existence out of soul material.
For you, it is just a fleeting hazy weaving;
For itself, it is beings feeling their soul denseness.
On earth they create with worldly understanding
In that ancient fiery ground that thirsts for forms.

THE SOUL OF FELIX BALD:

I do not want that their weight should burden me;
It'll create opposition to the impulse to float.

AHRIMAN

Your words are good. I'll grasp them quick,

So I may keep them unspoilt for myself;
You can't look after them any more yourself,
But on the earth you'd hate them.

THE SOUL OF STRADER (*a figure of which only the head is visible;
yellow-green aura with red and orange stars; right, far from the Soul of
Felix Bald*):
   Words audible in their echo and re-echo.
   They seem meaningful, but the sound is fading;
   Desire for an existence is taking hold of the re-echo.
   Which direction will it want to take?

THE OTHER PHILIA (*like a copy of Lucifer; but lacking the shining
of the under and over garments. Instead of the sword, a sort of dagger,
and instead of the planet, a red sphere like a piece of fruit*):
   Desiring weight, it draws onwards to the place
   Where that illumining existence is disappearing
   And as a hazy cloud of images
   Penetrates into the depths.
   If you preserve its meaning in your realm,
   I'll bear this force into that hazy cloud for you,
   Then on the earth you'll find it once again.

PHILIA (*angel-like figure, yellow lightening into whitish, with light
violet wings, a lighter shade than those Maria has later – all three soul
figures near to the Soul of Strader*):
   I'll cultivate the beings in that hazy cloud for you
   So all unknowingly they'll guide Will to you;
   Then I shall entrust it to the cosmic light
   Within which they create warmth for your being.

ASTRID (*angel-like figure, light violet mantel with blue wings*)

Blissfully I ray the bright life of the stars
To those beings so they may condense it into forms;
Far from knowledge, yet close to the heart's impulse,
They will give strength to your earthly body.

LUNA (*slender, angel-like figure, blue-red mantel with orange wings*):
In future I shall hide in your senses' body
The weighty being they create by weighing down,
Then, while thinking, you won't fashion it to evil
And thus unleash a storm within earth existence.

THE SOUL OF STRADER:
All three, they spoke in Sun-like, radiant words –
They are working within the circle of my sight, °
Creating figures for me, many in number;
I feel the impulse arising to meaningfully
Transform these through soul strength into a unity.
Awaken in me, you royal power of the Sun,
So I may dim you down through this opposition;
My desire brings it here from the Moon's sphere. –
Already a golden glow is aroused which feels warm,
And a cold silver glance that sprouts thoughts;
Glimmer on, O Mercury's passionate impulse,
Wed together my sundered cosmic existence.
- - - - - - - - - -
Now do I truly feel how a part of the image
I must here work up from cosmic spirit forces
Is again created for me.
(*Exit Ahriman.*)

THE SOUL OF CAPESIUS (*has appeared during Strader's first lines;
only the head is to be seen, which has a blue aura set with red and
yellow stars*):

At the far shoreline of my soul a picture
Is surfacing that has never touched my existence
Since I last wrested myself free of earthly life. It
Rays out blessings, in mildness works benevolently.
The warm radiance of wisdom streams from it,
And it grants my existence a clarifying light. – –
Could I but weave this image into a unity with myself
I would achieve what I have had to thirst for.
Yet I do not know what force could make
This picture active within my sphere.

LUNA:

What two earthly lives have given you, *feel* –
In ancient times the one flowed by
In earnest transformation; you lived through
A later one in dulling ambition; actively nourish
The latter with the blessed force of the former,
Then Jove's fire souls will reveal themselves
Within the circle of your sight.
You'll know yourself strengthened through wisdom.
That picture you are still looking on
At the far shoreline of your soul's sphere
Will then be able to move in close to you.

THE SOUL OF CAPESIUS:

Am I *really so indebted* to that soul preparing
Itself for existence that it admonishingly reflects
Itself as a picture within the circle of my soul?

ASTRID:

You are indeed; but it isn't yet calling on you
For redress in your next earthly life. –
This picture wants to give you thought forces
So as an individual you can find this human being
Who is showing you this picture of its earthly future.

THE OTHER PHILIA:

    The picture may well be allowed to come still nearer,
    But it may not penetrate into your own existence. –
    Therefore hold back its desire for your existence
    So you are able to come to the earth again
    Before it flows right into your own being.

THE SOUL OF CAPESIUS

    I feel *beforehand*, what I shall thank it for
    If I *want* to bring it still *closer* to me
    Yet can maintain myself independent of it.
    From Philia's realm I'm now beholding, in thoughtlike
    Images, the forces I'm to draw from its closeness.

PHILIA:

    When soon now Saturn of the many colors
    Rays forth its light upon you, use well the time;
    Through its force this picture of the one spiritually
    Related to you will plant into your soul sheaths the
    Roots of a thinking that is to uncover the meaning of
    Earthly development when that star again bears you.

THE SOUL OF CAPESIUS:

    The counsel you are giving me
    Shall guide me when Saturn shines upon me.

LUCIFER:

    Before they can leave this Sun Period
    With forces for their later earthly existence,
    I still want to awaken in these souls the sight
    Of worlds whose light will cause them pain.
    Sorrow must impregnate them with doubt.
    I shall summon up those spheres of soul
    They are not strong enough to look upon.

*(The Souls of Benedictus and Maria appear in the middle of
this domain. Benedictus, as a figure, is fashioned similar to the
configuration of the whole scenery, but in miniature. Widening out
towards the bottom, his mantel merges into blue-green; around his
head a red-yellow-blue aura is to be seen; the blue blends in with
the blue-green of the whole mantel. Maria as angel-like figure;
yellow blending into gold, without feet, with light-violet wings.)*

THE SOUL OF BENEDICTUS:

With your dense earth-burdened spheres, all of you
Are powerfully pressing upon my cosmic circle.
If you let this sense of self strengthen further,
Then you'll no longer find my Sun being
Raying into you in this spirit existence.

THE SOUL OF MARIA:

He was unknown to you all when last
You had to wear the garment of earthly matter;
Yet now is maturing within your soul sheaths
The force of those Sun words with which he
Benevolently cared for you in ancient earthly ages.
Fathom the deepest impulse of your beings,
Then you'll feel his closeness very strongly.

THE SOUL OF FELIX BALD:

Words are sounding forth from circles strange to me,
Yet no illumining existence produces those sounds
So for me they cannot be fully present as a being.

THE SOUL OF STRADER:

An illuming being is active at the spirit's shoreline,
Yet it is silent no matter how hard I try
To listen to the meaning of its illumining forces.

THE SOUL OF MRS. BALD *(the figure of a penitent, mantel of yellow-orange, waist cord of silver, she appears very near to Maria)*:
> You souls who Lucifer has just now summoned,
> The penitent hears the sound of your words
> Yet the Sun word alone is illumining him;
> Its *super-brilliance* is deadening your voices.
> The other one is beholding your starlight,
> Yet the star script is unknown to him.

THE SOUL OF CAPESIUS:
> The *star script!* – these words – they awaken thoughts;
> These words are bearing them to me on soul waves.
> Thoughts, that in a far-off earthly existence
> Were wonderfully revealed to my being.
> - - - - - - - - - -
> They illumine, yet they fade already while growing;
> Forgetfulness is spreading out its gloomy shadows.

THE GUARDIAN *(in symbolic robe, angel-like, approaching the Souls of Benedictus and Maria)*:
> You two souls that at Lucifer's command
> Approached the circle of these other souls,
> At this place you are within my power.
> The souls you are seeking – they seek you. –
> During this cosmic period, they in their spheres are
> Not to touch you by thoughts with their existence –
> Guard yourselves from penetrating into their circles.
> Should you venture it, it might harm you and them. –
> I'd have to weaken your starlight
> And banish you from them
> To the spheres of other realms for long cosmic ages.

(Curtain falls slowly.)

The spirit domain in the same style as the previous scene. The lighting warm and many shaded, but not too bright. Left, the Sylphs are standing. In front, Philia, Astrid, Luna. The Soul of Capesius, the Soul of Romanus, the Soul of Felix Bald; then the Souls of Torquatus and Bellicosus; the Other Philia with the Souls of Theodora and Mrs. Bald; later the Souls of Benedictus and Maria, the Guardian of the Threshold; Lucifer with the Soul of Johannes; at the end the Spirit of Johannes's Youth.

THE SOUL OF CAPESIUS (*standing on the right, towards the middle*):

> The picture that showed itself to me in my Sun Period,
> That rayed forth blessings, working goodness gently –
> It still holds sway within my being
> Even while the light of other wisdom now bathes
> This spirit region in its rays of many colors; but
> Even more is now becoming distinct from this picture;
> It wants me to draw out of it for future earthly ages
> What that soul, which is so significantly
> Revealing itself to my sphere in this picture,
> Once gave me during a sense existence together.
> Yet no stream of feelings
> Actively guides me to that soul.

THE SOUL OF ROMANUS (*a figure of which the whole upper part of the body down to the hips is to be seen, mighty red wings which so extend that they become transformed around the head into an aura that is red going over into blue on its outer edges; stands near to the Soul of Capesius; the Souls of Bellicosus and Torquatus are nearby*):

>   Arouse within yourself
> The image of the Jew who always heard only
> Hatred and scorn on every side, who nevertheless

Gave loyal service to that mystic brotherhood
With which you were once associated on earth.

THE SOUL OF CAPESIUS:
Now thought images begin to dawn that will to
Take hold of me with their strong power.
The picture of Simon is arising out of my soul tide. – –
But now draws near him still another – soul existence.
A penitent – could I but keep that one far from me.
(Felix Bald's Soul appears.)

THE SOUL OF ROMANUS:
Only during the period of the Cosmic Sun
Can he carry out his work here;
When Saturn is the illuminator of this spirit realm,
He wanders in solitude, shrouded in darkness.

THE SOUL OF CAPESIUS:
Oh, how this penitent now bewilders me. –
His soul rays are burning,
Boring themselves into my own soul sheaths. – –
This is how souls work who can behold other souls
In the deepest foundations of their being.

THE SOUL OF FELIX BALD *(with a muffled, as if veiled voice)*:
"My dear Keen, you always prove yourself true ..."

THE SOUL OF CAPESIUS:
I myself – my own words from him – –
As echo – sounding forth – in the spirit region!!
I will have to seek out this soul;
He knows me well – through him I must find myself.
*(Capesius's Soul disappears; from the left appears the "Other
Philia" with Theodora's Soul, behind her the Soul of Mrs. Bald.)*

THE SOUL OF ROMANUS:

>Two souls draw near to the penitent over there;
>The spirit who, through their love for it,
>These souls always acquire as guide strides on ahead.
>The light of gentleness issues from the one soul;
>It flows over to the other, who fashions herself
>Into a penitent for us. This image radiates
>Beauty's brilliance, which here lives on as wisdom.

THE SOUL OF TORQUATUS (*a figure visible to the chest, blue aura, green wings; speaking to the Soul of Capesius*):

>You are beholding the reflection of the longing
>I let ray out of my soul sheaths
>To your sphere in true spirit brotherhood.
>The primordial Rulers of Destiny have given me
>To you as activator of your mildness.
>Thus do souls spiritually serve other souls.
>Alone, in your stubborn mind, you'd never arrive
>At the gift of compassion in life.

THE SOUL OF BELLICOSUS (*a figure like the Soul of Torquatus, but blue-violet aura, blue-green wings*):

>Strengthen yourselves for spirit hearing; – the soul
>Now raying out in the light of gentleness, will speak.
>In Saturn's brilliance, this gloriously shining
>Sweet spirit blessedness is here coaxed from souls.

THE SOUL OF THEODORA (*angel-like figure, white with yellow wings and blue-yellow aura*):

>You, my true companion in the spirit,
>Let steam to him in gentle brilliance
>The love in your soul sheath –
>It will soothe his solitude's consuming fiery force –
>And guide to him here the rays of thought

From the souls of those shades there
Who are now gathering forces in the spirit worlds
So their soul bodies may livingly glimmer and thus
From the creation of their glimmering brilliance
A sense for growth and development may strengthen
For human souls in their life on earth.

THE SOUL OF MRS. BALD

You spirit in the appearance of a penitent, feel me;
Receive the force of the stars, you Sun soul. –
Until your spirit's sheath struggles free
From Lucifer's spell – I'll accompany you
Throughout your solitude and carry to you
The forces that I, wandering from star to star
In the cosmic all, shall gather in for you.

THE SOUL OF THEODORA:

Long past earthly thinking is aroused, flickering
There on my soul shoreline … a human image …
So I saw it in earthly form; it followed hither;
It re-echos here what once was heard then:
"The human soul arose from divine existence. Dying,
She can dive down into the foundations of her being.
One day she will release her spirit from death."
(*Lucifer and Thomasius's Soul appear during these last lines.*)

THE OTHER PHILIA (*first to the Soul of Theodora, then to the Soul of Mrs. Bald*):

This tone-emitting picture of beings bears hither
The active force from that noble brotherly love
You loyally unfolded upon the earth.
I shall transform it for you into soul strength.
The glimmering light of those shades is receiving
These words I am directing into your soul.

What they may now ponder on in eternity,
They will arouse for you in your earthly existence. –
And you, penitent of the Land of Spirits, °
Direct your soul steps to the stars.
The Daemons are longing for your work °
From which they'll ray forth *fantasy* into souls
And thus create wings for their life on earth.

THE SOUL OF MRS. BALD:

I'll follow you, you my sister soul,
You my Philia, who creates love,
From star to star, from one spirit to the next.
I'll follow you to the starry worlds,
I'll bear your words to many a cosmic sphere,
Fashioning *myself*, too, in these spirit activities
For my future earthly wanderings.
*(The Soul of Felix Bald, led by the Soul of Mrs. Bald, slowly
disappears; the Soul of Theodora remains standing rigid for a
while, looking on the Soul of Johannes; then she also disappears,
as does the Soul of Thomasius with Lucifer.)*

THE SOUL OF ROMANUS:

That at this spirit place we now have seen
The word of love and the word that creates
Come together in union, will strengthen
Within our selves the seeds we'll have need of
In our later earthly existence.
*(The Souls of Romanus, Torquatus, and Bellicosus disappear
– the Soul of Benedictus and the Soul of Maria appear at the side
of the Guardian of the Threshold.)*

THE GUARDIAN:

Recognize your Cosmic Midnight Hour!
I hold you both in the spell of that matured light

That Saturn now rays upon you until your sheaths,
Illumining your selves by the power of this light,
Can live its colors in stronger wakefulness.

THE SOUL OF MARIA:

The Cosmic Midnight Hour in wakefulness of soul? –
It was during the Moon Period that the Sun spoke
These solemn words of destiny: "The human souls who
Live through the Cosmic Midnight Hour in wakefulness
Behold a lightning that in quick blinding flashes
Illuminates future necessities in such a way
The spirit-glance dies in the recognition – –
And dying, forms itself into a sign of destiny
Forever actively etched into the soul."
Such souls hear thundering words
Dully rumbling in cosmic foundations,
Threatening all their soul delusions as it rolls.
(*Lucifer and the Soul of Thomasius appear again.*)

THE SOUL OF BENEDICTUS:

From the eternal, empty fields of ice penetrates
The call of destiny of our mystic friend. – –
If we can recognize the Cosmic Midnight Hour,
We will reach the spirit circle of his soul. °

THE SOUL OF MARIA:

Flames approach – they approach with my thinking –
There, from the cosmic shoreline of my soul;
A hot battle approaches – my own thinking –
It is battling with Lucifer's thoughts;
My own thinking battles within another soul – –
It draws forth a hot light – out of dark coldness. –
Like lightning blazes – this hot soul light – –
This soul's light – in the cosmic fields of ice.

LUCIFER:

    Recognize this light – my hot cosmic light –
    And look on the lightning that your own thinking
    Strikes – out of Lucifer's ruling circles.
    Since you are experiencing the Cosmic Midnight Hour,
    I bring within the circle of your vision
    That soul with whom you were long bound up.
    In future, if you wish to come near that soul,
    You'll have to change the direction of your seeking.
    You soul, you who have followed me here,
    Make use of the forces of the light that Saturn
    Rays forth into your Cosmic Midnight Hour. – –

THE SOUL OF JOHANNES (*angel-like figure, rose-red, without feet, with blue-red wings*):

    I am experiencing souls, but still need the power to
    Strengthen their light in me to that of a real being.
    Even when they're quite *close*, they still generate
    A thinking that only shines in the distance.
    How can I raise them into my spirit vision?

PHILIA:

    You will see them if you quickly grasp
    What they themselves illumine in the cosmic light;
    But when you look, use well the moment,
    For such illumination soon fades away.

THE SOUL OF JOHANNES:

    What the soul of that guide speaks to his pupil,
    That pupil's soul so close, so dear to me,
    It shall illuminate the circle of my soul.

THE SOUL OF BENEDICTUS:

    At this Spirit Midnight Hour

Create the Will you'll want to feel again
When the earth force arises for your form.
Your word, it will *illuminate* your friend's soul.

THE SOUL OF MARIA:

So may this word, that at this Cosmic Midnight Hour
I here entrust to the soul Lucifer has brought me,
May it grow strong within the cosmic light.
What is dear to me in the depths of my soul I shall
Look on, and looking on, shall speak, so that for
This soul it may be fashioned into a tone which
It may then feel within its own being in its
Earthly existence and so, lovingly bring it to life.
What then do I behold in my soul depths?
An exalted flaming script shines forth.
Love is flaming over to the soul of my guide,
Who in both earthly existence and in the spirit
Has accompanied me through the passage of long ages,
Who always found me when in earthly danger
The fervor of my prayers sought him, even when he
Himself tarried in spirit heights; shining brightly,
This love appears before me; ring out
You word of love from me to this other soul. – –
- - - - - - - - - -
But what flames are awoken by this word of love?
They illumine mildly, and the mildness rays out
Exalted earnestness; flashes of wisdom blaze
Through the cosmic ether, bestowing grace – –
And blessedness, weaving joy, is spreading out
Through the whole expanse of my soul circle.
O enduring time, I do entreat you:
Pour forth yourself into this blessedness
And let my guide, let this other soul,
Peacefully linger here, in you, with me.

THE GUARDIAN:

> So now may these flashes fade away to nothing
> That illuminate glaring future necessities
> When souls experience the Cosmic North awake.
> Now let the thunder lose its peel
> That warningly rolls at the Cosmic Midnight Hour. –
> To you, Astrid, a solemn command may now be given:
> Safeguard this soul thunder storm
> Until the next Cosmic Midnight Hour
> Finds this soul awakening in the stream of time.
> She shall then stand differently before her self – –
> Beholding her self in a picture of ancient times,
> Recognizing how even in the soul's downfall its wings
> Are strengthened for the flight to spirit heights.
> The soul must *never want to fall*,
> Yet it *must* take wisdom from its fall.

ASTRID:

> I shall safeguard the thunder and lightning's power
> So they may remain intact within cosmic existence
> Until Saturn once again inclines itself to this soul.

THE SOUL OF MARIA:

> I feel the stars' blessedness lingering on
> And may now enter it in the stream of time.
> With the soul so long bound up with me, I want to
> Live creating within the sway of this blessedness.

LUNA:

> I'll watch over your creating here in the spirit,
> So its fruits may ripen in your earthly existence.

THE SOUL OF JOHANNES:

> Within the circle of my soul – this star!

It shines forth blessings – rays forth grace –
A soul star – hovering – within the cosmic ether –
- - - - - - - - - -
But there – in subdued light – another star.
It is ringing out softly; yet I wish to hear it.
(With the last words the Spirit of Johannes's Youth appears.
Angel-like, silver light.)

THE SPIRIT OF JOHANNES'S YOUTH:

I nourish the existence of your desires with my life;
Illumining the goals of your youth,
My breath will become stronger when worlds
Into which I can joyfully lead you, tempt you.
When you lose me within yourself, I have to offer
My life to those shades with beingless existence.
O flower of my existence – do not leave me!

LUCIFER:

He won't leave you – in the depths of his being
I can see passions for light
That don't follow that other soul's trail. –
When these, with the brilliance they produce,
Strengthen themselves to existence
Within his soul foundations,
Then he won't want to squander the fruits
That they must produce in that realm
Where love wants to reign without beauty.

(Slow curtain.)

SCENE SEVEN

A temple approximately in Egyptian style. The site of an Initiation
lying far back in time. The Third Cultural Epoch of the earth. To
begin with, simply a conversation between the Hierophant of the
Sacrifice, the Threshold Guardian and the Mystic. °

THE HIEROPHANT OF THE SACRIFICE:
>Are all things worthily and rightly prepared
>My Threshold Guardian, so the holy rite may be
>Beneficial both for the Gods and for human beings.

THE THRESHOLD GUARDIAN:
>So far as a human being is capable of foreseeing,
>Everything is well prepared – sacred incense
>Has already filled the hall for many days.

THE HIEROPHANT OF THE SACRIFICE:
>My Mystic, the priest who is to receive
>The sacred revelation of secret wisdom today
>Is destined to be Counselor to the King.
>Have you then also fashioned his testing
>In such a way this Mystic is not solely devoted
>To the wisdom that attends only to the teachings
>Of the spirit without care for the earthly?
>Such a Counselor would be harmful for us.

THE MYSTIC:
>His testing was completed in a lawful manner,
>The Masters have accepted it as valid; – to me
>It seems this Mystic has only a limited sense
>For earthly cares; he has given up his soul
>Solely to spirit striving, to unfolding his self;
>One could see him as spirit enraptured. °

It's not too much to say he indulges himself
When his soul feels itself united with the spirit.

THE HIEROPHANT OF THE SACRIFICE:
You have really often seen him like this?

THE MYSTIC:
Truly, he often shows himself like this.
He would be better suited for
Inner Temple service than for your Counselor.

THE HIEROPHANT OF THE SACRIFICE:
That's enough. You go to your post
And take care our holy rite succeeds. —
(The Mystic exits.)
But you, my Guardian, hear me further.
You know I value your mystic gift;
As bearer of wisdom, for me you stand much higher
Than is in accord with your rank in the Temple,
And in your clairvoyant sight, I have often sought
For the test of my own spirit vision.
I ask you now, how great is your trust
In the spiritual ripeness of this new Mystic?

THE THRESHOLD GUARDIAN:
Who asks for my opinion;
My voice is not counted. —

THE HIEROPHANT OF THE SACRIFICE:
For myself, I always count it in.
Today, too, you are going to stand at my side;
We must follow this holy rite with a strictly
Exact soul vision, and if, for this Mystic,
His spirit experience is even the slightest bit

Inappropriate to the high sense of this ritual,
I shall prevent him from becoming Counselor.

THE THRESHOLD GUARDIAN:
What could be revealed with this new mystic
At this particular hallowed festival?

THE HIEROPHANT OF SACRIFICE:
I know he is not worthy of the honor
The Temple servants intend for him.
His human nature is well known to me.
For him, mysticism is not the heart's impulse
Aroused in a human being when in grace
Spirit light from above draws the soul to itself.
Passions are strongly burrowing away within him;
The impulses of the senses are not yet stilled.
Truly, I don't want to criticize the Will of the Gods,
Which in the stream of development
Wisely rays forth its light
Into the impulses and passions, too,
But when an impulse hides itself from its self
And mystically indulges in the mask of devotion,
Then it simply deceives thinking, falsifies the Will.
The light that weaves being in the spirit world
Does not penetrate into such a soul;
Passion defuses it as a mystic fog. °

THE THRESHOLD GUARDIAN:
My Hierophant, strict is the judgement
You place upon this man, who, young
And inexperienced, is not able to recognize his self,
Who can only conduct himself according to how the
Goal of the correct soul path is described by those
Who direct the sacrifice and lead the Mystics.

THE HIEROPHANT OF THE SACRIFICE:
  I do not wish to judge the man,
  I only want to judge the rite
  Taking place here at this holy solemn site.
  What we consummate as sacred mystic work
  Has significance not only here; right through the
  Words and deeds of this earnest sacrificial service
  Runs the stream of destiny of world events.
  What here takes place in an image,
  Creates eternally active existence in spirit worlds.
  But now, my Guardian, go to your work;
  You will discover for yourself
  How best you may help me during the service.
  (The Threshold Guardian exits left.)

THE HIEROPHANT OF THE SACRIFICE *(alone)*:
  It won't be the fault of this young Mystic,
  Who today wishes to offer himself to wisdom,
  If in the hours to come an unjustified feeling,
  Which could easily stream forth from his heart,
  Rays into our sacrificial rite and in the outer
  Image of deeds mystically approaches spirit spheres
  From which an unbeneficial effect will then
  Latter have to flow back into human life.
  Those leading and directing *will be guilty*.
  Do *they*, then, still recognize the mystic force
  That mysteriously and spiritually transfuses
  Every word and every gesture here – that also
  Has *effect* even when a soul content not beneficial
  For the world's development is poured into them?
  Instead of the young Mystic consciously offering
  Himself here to the spirit, his teachers drag him as
  Offering to this hallowed site, and here he will
  Unconsciously dedicate to the spirit a soul existence

He would actually direct along other pathways
If he were consciously able to live it *in* himself.
Within the circle of our mystic community,
Only the Most High Adept of the Sacrifice
Really recognizes what mystically lives
In the forms of the sacrifice;
Yet *he* is as silent as solitude,
For *such* is the strict law of his worthiness.
The others look on completely without understanding
When I speak of the earnestness of the sacrifice.
- - - - - - - - - -

Thus I am quite alone with my care,
A care that often oppresses me
When I feel the sense of this place of sacrifice.
Truly, here I learn to know it profoundly,
The solitude at this solemn spirit place.
Why am I at this place alone?
My soul must ask this – yet the spirit –
When will it give answer to *this* soul?

(*Curtain falls slowly.*)

SCENE EIGHT

The same temple scenery as in the seventh scene; to begin with
it is covered by a drop-curtain before which an Egyptian Woman
speaks the following. The Egyptian Woman is to be thought of as
one of the previous incarnations of Thomasius.

THE EGYPTIAN WOMAN:
      This is the hour at which he is consecrating
      His existence to serve the ancient, holy wisdom –
      And must tear himself away from me forever.
      Out of those heights of light, into which
      He is turning with *his* soul, will appear
      The Ray of Death for that of *mine*; without him –
      There is for me only grief, renunciation, sorrow
      To be found on the field of earth – and death. – –
      - - - - - - - - - -
      Though at this moment *he* is leaving me,
      Even so *I* wish to remain close to the place
      In which he is entrusting himself to the spirit.
      Might not I also behold with my own eyes
      How he will break free of the earth; – –
      Perhaps dream's revelation will let me
      Linger here, with him, in spirit insight.

*(The drop-curtain rises. We can see everything prepared for the
initiation of the Neophyte who is to be thought of as an earlier
incarnation of Maria; on one side of the sacrificial alter stands the
Most High Hierophant of the Sacrifice who is to be thought of as
an earlier incarnation of Benedictus; on the other side of the Alter,
the Keeper of the Words, an earlier incarnation of Hilary True-
to-God; somewhat in front of the altar, the Keeper of the Seals, an
earlier incarnation of Theodora; then on the one side of the altar
towards the front: the Representative of the Earth Element, an*

earlier incarnation of Romanus; the Representative of the Air
Element, an earlier incarnation of Magnus Bellicosus; very close
to the Most High Hierophant of the Sacrifice, the Hierophant
of the Sacrifice, an earlier incarnation of Capesius; on the other
side: the Representative of the Fire Element, an earlier incarnation
of Doctor Strader; the Representative of the Water Element,
an earlier incarnation of Torquatus. In front: Philia, Astrid,
Luna and the "Other Philia". Quite at the front in the figures of
Sphinxes: Lucifer and Ahriman; Lucifer such that the Cherub is
more emphasized, Ahriman such that the Bull is more emphasized.
Four other priests stand at the front. After the Temple hall with the
Mystics has become visible, a period of soundless stillness; then the
Threshold Guardian, an earlier incarnation of Felix Bald, and the
Mystic, an earlier incarnation of Mrs. Bald, lead the Neophyte in
through the gates on the left. They position him in the inner circle
close to the altar. They both remain standing near him.) °

THE THRESHOLD GUARDIAN:

From out of that shining web of semblance that °
You in the darkness of your error call world,
This Mystic has brought you hither to us. –
Woven out of existence and nothingness, the world in
Its weaving has fashioned itself into a shine for you.
That shine is good, when looked on from existence,
But you dreamed it within a life of shine, and a
Shine discerned from a shine sinks out of the all. –
You, shine of a shine, learn to recognize yourself.

THE MYSTIC:

So speaks the one who guards this Temple's Threshold,
Experience the heavy weight of this word within you.

THE REPRESENTATIVE OF THE EARTH ELEMENT:

Within the heavy weight of this earth existence,

Fearlessly grasp the shine of your own being
So you can sink into world depths. – –
In world depths, seek for existence in the darkness;
Bind what you find there to your shine;
In weighing down, it will bestow existence on you.

THE KEEPER OF THE WORDS: Understanding
Of where we are leading you in this sinking
Will first come to you when you follow out his word.
We are forging the form of your own being;
Recognize our work, otherwise you'll have to totally
Dissolve yourself as a shine within world nothingness.

THE MYSTIC:
So speaks the one who guards this Temple's Words,
Experience the heavy weight of these words within you.

THE REPRESENTATIVE OF THE AIR ELEMENT:
Flee from the heavy weight of this earth existence;
It deadens the existence of your self in its sinking.
Fly from it with the lightness of air. –
In world widths, seek existence in the luminous light;
Bind what you find there to your shine;
In the flight, it will bestow existence on you.

THE KEEPER OF THE WORDS: Understanding
Of where we are leading you in this flight
Will first come to you when you follow out his word.
We are illuminating the life of your being;
Recognize our work, otherwise you'll have to totally
Dissolve yourself as a shine within world weight.

THE MYSTIC:
So speaks the one who guards this Temple's Words,

Experience the wing'd force of these words within you.

THE MOST HIGH HIEROPHANT OF THE SACRIFICE:
My son, on this noble path of wisdom, you are to
Follow the words of these Mystics literally. –
You cannot behold their answer within yourself,
For dark error is still weighing down on you, and
Within you, folly strives towards cosmic distances.
Therefore, look – into this flame, which is closer
(The brightly illumining, leaping, sacrificial flame flares up on the altar standing in the middle.)
To you than the life of your own being,
And read the answer for yourself from the fire.

THE MYSTIC:
So speaks the one who guides this Temple's Sacrifice,
Experience the holy force of this sacrifice within you.

THE REPRESENTATIVE OF THE FIRE ELEMENT:
Let the error of your sense of self burn away
In the fire flaring up within this sacrifice.
Burn away your self with the material of your error. –
Within world fire, seek your existence as flame;
Bind what you find there to your shine.
In the burning up, it will bestow existence on you.

THE KEEPER OF THE SEALS: Understanding
Of why we are fashioning you into a flame
Will first come to you when you follow out his word.
We are purifying the form of your own being;
Recognize our work, otherwise you'll have to
Lose yourself without form within world water.

THE MYSTIC:
So speaks the one who guards this Temple's Seals,

Experience the illumining power of wisdom within you.

THE REPRESENTATIVE OF THE WATER ELEMENT:
Prevent the flaming power of the world of fire
From consuming your rule over your own existence.
This shine won't become an existence for you
Unless the beat of the waves of world water
Can penetrate you with the tone of the spheres.
Seek your existence as wave in world water;
Bind what you find there to your shine.
In the surging, it will bestow existence on you.

THE KEEPER OF THE SEALS: Understanding
Of why we are fashioning you as a wave
Will first come to you when you follow out his word.
We are fashioning the form of your own being;
Recognize our work, otherwise you'll have to
Lose yourself without form within world fire.

THE MOST HIGH HIEROPHANT OF THE SACRIFICE:
My son, with a strong power of Will, you are also
To follow the words of these mystics correctly.
You cannot behold the answer in yourself.
Your power is still frozen in cowardly fear;
You cannot fashion this weakness into the wave that
Lets yourself ring out in the realm of the spheres.
Therefore, listen to your soul's forces speaking,
Recognize your own voice within its word.

PHILIA:
Purify yourself in the fire – – as world wave
Lose yourself in the tone of the spirit spheres.

ASTRID:
Fashion yourself in the tone of the spirit spheres –

Light as air fly into world distances.

LUNA:

With earthly heaviness, sink into world depths;
Embolden yourself as self within heavy weight.

THE OTHER PHILIA:

Distance yourself from your own existence;
Unite yourself with the power of the elements.

THE MYSTIC:

So speaks *your own* soul within the Temple,
Experience in it the directing power of these forces.

THE MOST HIGH HIEROPHANT OF THE SACRIFICE:

Companion Hierophant, this soul,
Whom we are to lead onto the path of wisdom,
Fathom it in its depths – make known to us
What you can behold as its present state.

THE HIEROPHANT OF THE SACRIFICE:

What our sacrifice ordains, has come about.
The soul has forgotten what it was.
The oppositions of the elements
Have swept away its shining web of error
Which now lives on in the strife of the elements.
The soul has preserved only its being,
And what lives in its being, it shall read
In the world word that speaks out of the flame.

THE MOST HIGH HIEROPHANT OF THE SACRIFICE:

So read, O human soul, what the flame makes known
To you as the world word within your inner being.
- - - - - - - - - -

(There occurs a long pause while it becomes completely dark, –

only the flame and the indefinite outlines of the people are to be
seen; the Most High Hierophant continues on after the pause;)
And *now* awaken from world vision!
Make know what is to be read within the word.
(The Neophyte is silent. The Most High Hierophant continues on
disconcerted:)
He is silent!
Has what you have beheld disappeared? – Speak!

THE NEOPHYTE:
Obedient to your strict words of the sacrifice,
I sank myself into this living being of flame
Awaiting the tone of the higher world words.
(The assembled mystics, except the Hierophant of the Sacrifice,
display an ever increasing horror during the speech of the
Neophyte.)
I felt how with the lightness of air
I was able to free myself from earthly weight. – –
Lovingly taken up by world fire,
I felt myself in streaming waves of spirit.
I saw how the form of my earthly life
Maintained itself as another being outside me. – –
Though wrapped in blessedness, though feeling myself
In spirit light, even so I could only contemplate my
Earthly covering with an interest filled with desire. – –
Spirits of the higher worlds rayed light upon it; – –
The beings that actively care for its life
Approached it like butterflies, sparkling brightly. °
From the glittering light of those beings,
My body rayed back a sparkling play of colors
That could be seen flashing near, glowing further off
And at last was lost scattered in space.
Within that spirit-soul existence, the desire
Sprang up that earthly weight might sink me down

Into my sheath so that through feeling I could
Cultivate a sense of joy within life's warmth. – –
Joyfully diving down into my sheath,
I sensed your strict call to awaken.

THE MOST HIGH HIEROPHANT OF THE SACRIFICE (*himself
disconcerted to the disconcerted Mystics*):
This is not something seen in spirit –
An earthly feeling – has wrung itself free from this
Mystic and mounted as sacrifice into the bright
Spirit heights – oh sacrilege, sacrilege! – –

THE KEEPER OF THE WORDS (*in anger to the Hierophant*):
This wouldn't have been possible had you administered
The office entrusted to you as Hierophant of the
Sacrifice in the sense of its ancient sacred duties.

THE HIEROPHANT OF THE SACRIFICE:
In this celebration I have carried out what
Has been laid upon me as duty by higher realms.
I have abstained from thinking the words
Enjoined upon me according to custom
And that were supposed to work in spirit
From my thinking over to the Neophyte.
Thus the young man had no one else's thinking;
He has made known his own being here.
Truth has triumphed. – You may punish me;
I had to do what you have experienced in fear.
I already feel the times are drawing near
Which will liberate the I from the group spirit
And set its own thinking free for it.
It may be this young man will now wrest himself free
Of your mystic path. – A later earthly existence
Will certainly show him the ways of the Mystics
Foreseen for him by the Powers of Destiny.

THE MYSTICS:

O sacrilege

– that calls for atonement

– for punishment –

(The Sphinxes begin to speak one after the other as Ahriman and Lucifer; until now they were motionless like statues; what they say is heard only by the Hierophant, the Most High Hierophant and the Neophyte; – the others remain agitated by the preceeding events.)

AHRIMAN AS SPHINX:

I must take captive for my own site what here
Wants to come to light in an unjust manner.
I'll then have to foster it further in darkness;
It should thence create in spirit the ability
To advantageously weave itself
With a right sense for development into human life;
But until this ability becomes effective,
What here proves to be an earthly burden
For this holy service, will serve my work.

LUCIFER AS SPHINX:

I shall carry off for my own site what here
As spirit desire delights in the shine.
As shine it will joyfully sparkle within my light
And in this way be consecrated in spirit to that
Beauty still wanting to hold the heaviness of earthly
Weight distant from it at this time. In beauty,
This shine will be transformed into existence;
It will then in future be the light of the earth –
Sinking down as light that flees from here.

THE MOST HIGH HIEROPHANT OF THE SACRIFICE:

The Sphinxes are speaking –
They, that were only images

Since the Hierophants first performed this rite here,
The spirit, it has grasped dead form – –
Oh destiny, you are sounding forth as world word! – –

*(The other mystics, except for the Hierophant and the Neophyte,
are astounded by the words of the Most High Hierophant.)*

THE HIEROPHANT OF THE SACRIFICE *(to the Most High
Hierophant):*

What we consummate as sacred mystical work
Has significance not only here; right through the
Words and deeds of this earnest sacrificial service
Runs the stream of destiny of world events.

(On the mood aroused by the preceeding events, the curtain falls.)

SCENE NINE

A small room presenting a pleasant but serious mood – like a study – in the house of Hilary. – To begin with Maria alone in meditation; then Astrid appears, later Luna, the Guardian of the Threshold and Benedictus.

MARIA:

A soul star, there, at the shoreline of the spirit –
It is approaching – approaching in spirit brightness,
It is approaching with my self – as it approaches –
Its light is gaining in strength – in calmness, too.
You star within my spirit horizon, what is –
Your approach raying out to my soul vision?
(Astrid appears.)

ASTRID:

Recognize what I am permitted to bestow on you.
From the cosmic battle of the light with darknesses,
I separated out the power of your thinking.
From your awakening at the Cosmic Midnight Hour,
I loyally bring it back into your earthly form.

MARIA:

Until now, my Astrid, you have only ever
Appeared to me as an illuminating soul shade;
What has made you into a bright spirit star for me?

ASTRID:

The force of thunder and lightning I received from you
So they would remain preserved in your soul existence –
And so you could now behold them with understanding –
When you bring back to mind the Cosmic Midnight Hour.

MARIA:

> The Cosmic Midnight Hour! – before the sheath
> For this earthly life enclosed my self –
> Watched through in Saturn's colored light!
> Until now my earthly thinking has sheathed
> That spirit experience in soul mirkiness – –
> Now it is climbing up into soul brightness. – –

ASTRID:

> In the cosmic light, you yourself spoke these words:
> "O enduring time, I do entreat you:
> Pour forth yourself into this blessedness
> And let my guide, let this other soul,
> Peacefully linger here, in you, with me."

MARIA:

> Linger also you, O present moment, with me,
> You who are allowed to create what happens in spirit
> As a force within my self. Fortify my soul
> So you do not pass away like a dream.
> In the light that illumined the Cosmic Midnight Hour,
> That Astrid creates out of my soul mirkiness,
> My I unites itself to that self that created me
> For service to itself within the great Cosmic Being.
> Yet how shall I hold onto you, O present moment,
> So I do not lose you when the senses once again
> Experience the earth's brightness around me?
> For great is their strength; they deaden
> What is seen in spirit – often enough it is also
> Dead when the self finds itself again in spirit.
> *(With the last words, as if called out by them, Luna appears)*

LUNA:

> Before sense existence makes you dream again,

Preserve for yourself the power of Will
This moment is allowed to create.
Bring to mind the words I myself spoke
When you saw me at the Cosmic Midnight Hour.

MARIA:

You, my Luna, have brought this *power of Will*
Out of the Cosmic Midnight Hour here to me
As support in this earthly existence.

LUNA:

My words followed on the Guardian's warning:
"You will now stand differently before your self,
Beholding your self in a picture of ancient times,
Recognizing how even in the soul's downfall its wings
Are strengthened for the flight to spirit heights;
The soul must *never want to fall,*
Yet it must take wisdom from its fall."
- - - - - - - - - -

MARIA:

To where is the power of your words carrying me off?
A spirit star, there, at the shoreline of the soul! –
It is shining – is approaching – as a spirit figure;
Its light is gaining in density. – Forms, darkening °
In the light, turning themselves into beings! –
A young mystic, a sacrificial flame,
The strict command of the Most High Hierophant
To make known literally the contents of that flame!
- - - - - - - - - -

The circle of Mystics in horror, completely confused
At that young Mystic's self-acknowledgement!
(The Guardian of the Threshold appears during the last lines.)

501

THE GUARDIAN:

Fathom still further within your spirit listening
The Most High Hierophant's strict command.

MARIA:

"So read, O human soul, what the flame makes known
To you within the world word as your inner being."
Who spoke these words my own thinking, remembering,
Carries to me from those flooding tides of soul?
(Benedictus appears after the first sentence.)

BENEDICTUS:

With my own words you have called me to you. –
When ages ago I commanded you in these words,
You were not found ready to be my follower.
They then rested in the lap of world events. °
The long course of ages has bestowed on them the
Power that flowed to it from the life of your soul;
They thus worked on in your later lives on earth
Unconsciously within the depths of your soul.
Now they let you find me once again as guide.
Consciously, in thought, they recreate themselves
Into a strong content for your life.
"What we consummate as sacred mystical work
Has significance not only here; right through the
Words and deeds of this earnest sacrificial service
Runs the stream of destiny of world events."

MARIA:

You did not speak *these* words at that place.
The Hierophant spoke them, he who was
Your companion in that ancient mystic brotherhood.
Already at that time it was known to him
The Powers of Destiny were foreseeing the end

Of that brotherhood. – Unconsciously, the Hierophant
Was looking out on the beautiful, faint shining glow
Just dawning over Hellas heralding
A new sun for the spiritual stream of the earth.
So it was he suppressed those powers of thought
He should have directed into my soul.
He served as instrument for the Cosmic Spirit
Within the hallowed work through which
He heard the stream of world events whispering.
He spoke words from his deepest soul foundations,
"Truly, here I learn to know it profoundly,
The solitude at this solemn spirit place.
Why am I at this place alone?"

BENEDICTUS:

Thus was laid in his soul the germ of the impulse
For *solitude;* in the lap of time
That seed kernel has ripened into soul fruit.
Capesius now experiences this fruit as a Mystic;
It impels him to follow the example of Felix.

MARIA:

Yet that woman who took her stand by the Temple;
I see her in that ancient time,
But my vision does not yet penetrate
Into her present time; how can I find her
When sense existence makes me dream again?

THE GUARDIAN:

                              You will find her
When in the realm of souls you look upon
That being she divines as a shade among shades.
She strives towards it with a strong soul force.
She will be able to free it from the realm of shades

If in her present life she can first behold
Her long-past earthly existence through you.
(The Guardian of the Threshold and Benedictus disappear.)

MARIA:

As illumining soul star, the earnest Guardian
Wafts away towards the shoreline of my soul. –
His illumination spreads calmness far into the widths –
Sublimeness rays out from him – his earnestness
Pours strength into my being's deepest foundations. –
I shall submerge myself in this calmness – –
I divine that through it I will be able
To guide myself to full spirit wakefulness.
I shall maintain you both, you my soul messengers – –
As shining stars in my existence. – –
On you, Astrid, I will call when thoughts want
To disengage themselves from the soul's brightness. –
And from you, O Luna, may my words come to me
When the power of Will sleeps in my soul depths. –

(The curtain falls while Maria, Astrid and Luna are still in the room.)

SCENE TEN

The same room as in the ninth scene. To begin with, Johannes alone meditating. The Other Philia, Maria, The Spirit of Johannes's Youth, Lucifer, Benedictus.

JOHANNES:

"This is the hour at which he is consecrating
His existence to serve the ancient, holy wisdom; –
Perhaps dream's revelation will let me
Linger here, with him, in spirit insight."
Thus spoke in ancient times near the Temple
The woman I now behold in a spirit picture;
And thinking of her, I feel myself strengthened.
What is this image doing to me? What in this vision
Is holding me to it, as if firmly spellbound? Truly,
It is not an interest that from the image itself °
Forces itself on me; for if it came before my eyes
As a picture in sense existence, it wouldn't seem
To have any content. What is speaking out of it?
(The voice of the "Other Philia" as if from afar.)

THE OTHER PHILIA:

The enchanted weaving
Of this their own being.

JOHANNES:

And awakened dreaming
To souls is revealing
The enchanted weaving
Of this their own being.
(While Johannes is speaking these lines, the "Other Philia" comes towards him.)

JOHANNES:

Who are you, enigmatic enchanting spirit?
You brought true counsel into my soul –
And yet at the same time deceived me about *yourself*.

THE OTHER PHILIA:

Johannes, this double aspect of your being
You created out of yourself. Just as shades
Encircle you, so must *I*, too,
Until you *yourself* set free that shade
Your guilt creates a spellbound life for.

JOHANNES:

For the third time – you speak these words;
I want to follow them. – Show me the way.

THE OTHER PHILIA:

Johannes, seek for what, living within the spirit's
Light, has been preserved for you within your self.
It will give you light from its light.
You will then be able to behold in your self
How you may wipe out your debt in a later life.

JOHANNES:

How shall I seek for what, living within the spirit's
Light, has been preserved for me within my self?

THE OTHER PHILIA:

Give me what you yourself are when thinking of
Yourself; lose yourself for but a short time in me,
Yet so, that you will *not* be another for yourself.

JOHANNES:

How can I give myself to you without first
Beholding you in your true being?

THE OTHER PHILIA:

    I am in you, am a part of your soul.
    I myself am the force of love within you,
    The hopes of your heart active within you,
    The fruit of long past earthly lives
    Preserved for you within your existence.
    Oh, look on them through me – feel me,
    And then look on your self through my power in you.
    Fathom within yourself the being in the picture
    That created for you that vision without interest.
    (The Other Philia disappears.)

JOHANNES:

    O enigmatic spirit, I can feel you within me,
    Yet I cannot behold you any longer.
    Where do you dwell within me?
    (The call of the "Other Philia", as if from afar.)

THE OTHER PHILIA:

    The enchanted weaving
    Of this their own being.

JOHANNES:

    The enchanted weaving
    Of this their own being.
    Enchanted weaving of this my own being,
    Fathom within me the being of that picture
    That my vision without interest created for me.
    - - - - - - - - - -
    To where is the power of these words carrying me off?
    A spirit star, there, at the shoreline of my soul –
    It is shining, is approaching – as a spirit figure;
    As it approaches growing brighter – forms take shape –
    They are alive, active, like individual persons –
    A young mystic – a sacrificial flame.

The strict command of the Most High Hierophant
To make known literally the contents of that flame. –
- - - - - - - - - -
The young mystic sought by that woman who my vision
Created for itself in a picture without interest.
(Maria appears as a thought figure of Johannes's.)

MARIA:

Who thought on thee before the sacrifical flame?
Who felt you near the sacred place?
Johannes, if you want to tear your spirit shade
Out of those enchanted worlds of soul,
Then live the goals shining on you from it.
The trail on which you're seeking is leading you on,
But first you must find it again in the right way.
The woman near the Temple shows it to you
When she is powerfully living in your thoughts.
She is striving, enchanted among the shadow spirits,
Towards that other shade who, through you,
Now performs evil service for those cruel shades.
(The Spirit of Johannes's Youth appears.)

THE SPIRIT OF JOHANNES'S YOUTH:

I want to always be united with you in future
If you will lovingly nurture the forces
Loyally preserved for me in the lap of time
From that ancient age by the young Mystic
Whom your soul once sought at the Temple;
However, you must also behold in its truth
The spirit at whose side I have now appeared.

MARIA:

Maria, as you have wished to behold her,

She is not in worlds where truth shines forth.
My holy solemn vow rays forth the force
That shall preserve for you what you have won.
You will find me in those bright fields of light
Where beauty radiantly creates the forces of life:
Seek me in those cosmic foundations where souls
Want to battle to win what the gods feel by means of
That love the self beholds in the world all.
(Lucifer appears while Maria speaks the last line.)

LUCIFER:

So work compelling Rulers,
So feel Spirits of the Elements,
The forces of your Master
And make plain the way,
So from earth's domain
Can now be directed
Into Lucifer's realm
What my desire longs for,
What obeys my Will.
(Benedictus appears.)

BENEDICTUS:

Maria's holy solemn vow is now working
Its healing radiance within his soul.
He will value you, but not succumb to you.

LUCIFER:

I mean to fight.

BENEDICTUS:

And fighting serve the gods.

(Curtain falls.)

SCENE ELEVEN

The same room as in both the foregoing scenes. Bendictus and Strader enter the room:

STRADER:

> You spoke earnest, and Maria
> Very hard words as well, when you both
> Showed yourselves to me at my life's abyss.

BENEDICTUS:

> You know those images have no real being;
> The content is what wants to enter the soul
> And to reveal itself in an image.

STRADER:

> Yet what spoke out of those images was hard,
> "Where is your light? You're raying out darkness. You
> Are conveying your confusing darkness into the light."
> So spoke the spirit, even if in Maria's image.

BENEDICTUS:

> Since you on your road to the spirit
> Have raised yourself one stage higher,
> The spirit leading you upwards to itself has
> Declared everything previously achieved as darkness.
> That spirit selected Maria's image
> Because your soul formed it thus for yourself.
> My dear Strader, that spirit is now powerfully ruling
> Within yourself; it is leading you on
> In hurried flight to higher stages of your soul.

STRADER:

> And yet quite terrifyingly rings out to my soul,

"Because you're too cowardly to ray out your own
Light." This the spirit in that picture also spoke.

BENEDICTUS:

That spirit did, indeed, have to call you cowardly,
Because what is bravery for lesser souls
Really is cowardly for your soul.
In our progress, what was formerly courage
Becomes a cowardliness which must be overcome.

STRADER:

Oh, how these words affect me!
Romanus spoke to me recently of his plan.
I shouldn't carry out my project
In unity with you, rather without your help.
He'd then be ready to stand by Hilary
With everything he possesses. –
On the basis of my objection I would
Never separate this work from your circle,
He then declared that further efforts
Were in vain. Romanus is supporting
The opposition Hilary's companion is putting up
To this plan, without which my life must
Really seem completely worthless to me.
Since these two men are now tearing my field of
Action out from under me, I can see nothing before me
But a life where the very air for living fails.
In order that the flight of my spirit
Is not lamed by this, I'll need that courage
You just spoke of. – But whether
I shall also show myself strong enough,
That I'm not capable of saying, for I feel
How the force I want to unleash is also
At the same time turning destructively against me.

BENEDICTUS:

    Maria and Johannes have just newly progressed
    In their clairvoyant vision; what had previously
    Still hindered them from taking the step
    From the mystic life into sense existence,
    Is no longer present; in the further course of time,
    Goals will be found for you and them together. –
    Not as guides, but as actual creators of forces
    Are these words of the Mystics to be valued:
    What must happen, will happen.
    Therefore, in wakefulness let us await
    In what way the spirit will show us its signs.

STRADER:

    A short while ago a picture formed
    I have to see as a sign of destiny.
    I was on a ship, at the helm, *you;*
    I had to tend to the rudder mechanism.
    We were piloting Maria and Johannes
    To their work site; then another ship
    Appeared quite close to us; in it
    Were Romanus with the friend of Hilary.
    They lay athwart our course as enemies.
    I had to battle against them; then Ahriman
    Entered the battle on their side.
    Now I saw myself in a hard fight with him;
    At my side came to my help Theodora.
    Then the image disappeared from my spirit horizon. –
    Before Capesius and Felix I once ventured to utter
    The words, "I would easily bear the opposition
    Now threatening my work from without;
    Even if my acts of Will shattered on it, –
    I'd be capable of maintaining myself." –
    Does this picture now want to indicate to me

That the outer opposition is but the expression
Of an inner battle – of a fight with Ahriman?
Am I then armed for *this* battle as well?

BENEDICTUS:

My friend, I can behold within your soul
How this image has not yet fully ripened for you.
I feel you are capable of strengthening the force
That placed this image before your spirit eye. –
I can now perceive you will create forces
For yourself and also for your friends if you
Will to correctly strive for this strengthening.
I can feel all this; yet how it will work out,
Lies hidden from my sight.

(Curtain falls.)

SCENE TWELVE

The interior of the earth. Enormous crystal formations broken up by lava-like flows; the whole thing in subdued lighting, in part transparent, in part translucent. Towards the top, red flames as if pressed downwards together by the roof.

AHRIMAN (at first alone):

    The left-over junk of a being is falling from above, °
    And I must make use of it. Such daemonic stuff
    Passes away in this region of forms. An individual
    Is striving to totally root out of its being
    The spirit substance it has received from me.
    Up to this point, I could inspire it reasonably well,
    Yet now it's far too close to that swarm of Mystics
    Who through Benedictus's light of wisdom
    Could defiantly obtain wakefulness at the
    Cosmic Midnight Hour. They, Lucifer has
    Forfeited, thus Maria and Johannes
    Could slip away from the region of his light.
    Now I'll have to take a tenacious hold on Strader.
    Once I have him though, I'll get the others, too.
    Johannes has already blunted himself dreadfully
    On my shadow – he knows me well.
    Without Strader, though, I can't get at him,
    And with Maria, it's the same;
    But maybe Strader won't quite yet be able to see
    All that spiritual confusion human beings
    Take for Nature as just my spirit gear
    And will suppose a blind web of energy and material
    Where I spiritually create by denying the spirit.
    Certainly the others have gossiped plenty to him
    About my individuality and my realm,

But I don't see him as quite lost yet.
He'll forget Benedictus sent him here
With partial understanding in order to drive
Out of him the belief I'm nothing
But something spun in the brain of human heads. °
Only, I'll need earthly help if I'm to lure
Him into my domain at the right moment.
I'm going to call a soul to me now
Who deems himself so clever that for him
I'm nothing but a stupid deception of fools.
He serves me now and then, when I can use him. –
(Ahriman exits, comes back with the Soul of Renard Fox; in its
figure, it is sort of a copy of Ahriman; on entering, he takes a
blindfold from the eyes of the person who is portraying the Soul.)

AHRIMAN:

Earthly intelligence he's had to leave at the door.
He's certainly not to understand what he's
To experience with me; for he's still honest,
And he wouldn't do anything for me if he understood
What I'm now going to inspire him to.
He also must be able to forget it later on.
- - - - - - - - - -
Do you know Doctor Strader, who serves me? °

THE SOUL OF RENARD FOX

He roams about on that Earth Star.
He'd like to build his learned prattle into life,
But every social gale just blows it down.
He listens greedily to those mystic snobs.
He's already half smothered in their foggy haze,
And now he wants to befog Hilary.
He'll be reined in though, by Hilary's friend,

Since otherwise that bunch of charlatans'd utterly
Destroy the firm with all their spirit dribble.

AHRIMAN:

Such chatter does not serve me.
I need Strader now. – So long as this man
Can have complete faith in *himself*,
It'll be far too easy for Benedictus to succeed
In getting his wisdom across to those people.
That friend of Hilary has been able to serve Lucifer
Quite well; I, however, must strive otherwise. –
Through Strader I must weaken Benedictus.
If *he* does not have Strader, he'll accomplish
Nothing more with his other pupils.
It's true, my opponents still have their power;
After Strader's death, they'll have him.
If I, however, can still disconcert this soul
Within *itself* while here on earth,
It would mean Benedictus could no longer
Use him as a frontman for himself.
Now I've already read in the Book of Destiny
How Strader's life has just about run its course.
This Benedictus cannot see. – –
My loyal knave, you're almost too crafty; °
You believe I'm a stupid fantasy of fools.
You reason so well a person can even hear you. °
So go to Strader in a bit, make it clear to him
His mechanism's no good, that it's not simply due
To unfavorable times that he can't hold to what
He's promised, that he's ill-conceived it.

THE SOUL OF RENARD FOX:

For that I've been well prepared. For long
All my pondering's been directed towards

How I can correctly prove to Strader
He's given himself up to error's ways.
When, over many nights, one has first
Cleverly invented such junk as that in thought,
One can easily believe the failure may lie
Not in the thinking itself, that it could only come
From without. But with Strader it's really pitiful.
Had *he* kept himself outside that mystic fog and
Made use of his clever understanding and good sense,
The very greatest advantages would certainly
Have accrued to humanity from his lofty gifts.

AHRIMAN:

You're now to arm yourself well with cleverness.
Your work is to be: that Strader will no longer
Want to find the right belief within his self.
Then in future he'll also no longer want
To stand by Benedictus; he, in turn, will then
Have to rely upon himself and *his own* reasons;
But those are not so pleasant for some people.
They'll be the more hated on the earth,
The more truthfully they're able to be shown.

THE SOUL OF RENARD FOX:

Now it comes to me, how I can demonstrate
To Strader the failure in his thinking.
His mechanism has a fault
He himself's not able to make clear to himself.
The Mystics' darkness hinders him.
With my rationality, I'll actually be able
To perform much better service for him.
I've wanted to do this for a long time already
But didn't know how I should go about it.
Now, finally, I feel *enlightened* about it.

I must take a good look at everything
That could convince Strader of the truth.
*(Ahriman leads Renard's soul out of his domain, again tying the
blindfold over the eyes of the person portraying this soul before he
leaves.)*

AHRIMAN *(alone)*:

He'll be able to perform good service for me.
The Mystics' light on earth is really burning me.
I must be able to work further there,
But without those Mystics revealing my work.
(Theodora appears.)

THE SOUL OF THEODORA:

You may be capable of getting at Strader,
But *I* am at his side. Ever since he found me
On that bright soul path, he has been united °
With me, whether leading his life
In the spirit domain or in the earthly realm.

AHRIMAN:

If she really doesn't leave him as long as
He is lingering on the earth, the fight will be lost;
But I can certainly still hope that even so,
He may yet forget her in the end.

(Curtain falls.)

A large reception room in Hilary's house. As the curtain opens,
Hilary and Romanus are together in conversation; later Capesius,
Felix Bald, the Secretary; Philia.

HILARY:

It's painful to have to say it, dear friend,
But for me the knot of destiny forming
Here within our circle is all but crushing.
On what can one build when everything is shaky?
Through you, Benedictus's friends
Are held back from our goal; Strader is now
Weighed down with bitter agonies of doubt. –
A man, who with shrewdness and with – hatred has
Often set himself against the Mystics' striving,
Has been able to prove to Strader
He has profoundly erred with his mechanism,
That it's not possible in itself,
Not simply blocked by outer opposition. –
No fruit has ripened for me from this life;
I have longed for deeds – yet the thoughts
That could mature them I have always lacked.
This soul desolation torments me most bitterly.
Only my spirit vision has held me upright,
And yet – it could deceive me about Strader.

ROMANUS:

Very often, when your words were shown to be
In serous error by the course events took
And so your spirit vision seemed like a deception,
I felt as if a nightmare were
Weighing down on my soul most painfully.
That nightmare has become my inner mystic teacher;

It has set free a feeling within me
Which can now illuminate my judgement of all this. –
You have trusted spirit vision much too blindly,
Thus it can appear to you as error, just there, where
It would certainly lead you to what is true.
With Strader, you've seen quite correctly, in spite
Of everything that all too clever man could prove. °

HILARY:

So your faith isn't shaken a bit; you firmly
Hold to the opinion you had of Strader?

ROMANUS:

I have, in fact, formed it on the basis of reasons
Having nothing to do with Strader's friends,
And these reasons stand, whether his mechanism
Is shown to be correct or faulty.
Even if he has deceived himself about it,
Still, a person must find the truth through error.

HILARY:

The lack of success doesn't disturb you –
You, whom life has always brought only success?

ROMANUS:

Those have success who fear no failure.
However, we must also understand mysticism
In its appropriate sense for this case, and it
Shows us quite clearly what to think of Strader.
He'll be able to prove himself victor
In the fight to open the spirit gates;
He will boldly stride by that watchman
Who stands before the Threshold of the Spiritland.
I have felt penetrating through my whole soul
Those words of the strict Guardian at the Threshold. –

I intuit him at Strader's side right now.
Whether Strader *beholds* him, or approaches him
Unconsciously, I truly cannot fully fathom;
But I believe I know Strader well enough.
With courage, he will turn towards the insight
Self-knowledge must beget pain.
That Will that bravely gives itself over to
The future will then become a companion for him, and
Strengthened by the forces at the well-spring of hope,
It will set itself over against the pain of knowledge.

HILARY:

For these mystic words, have thanks my friend.
I've heard them often enough before, yet only now
Am I able to feel what they secretly contain.
Only with difficulty are cosmic pathways fathomable,
And for me, my dear friend, it behooves me to wait
Until the spirit wants to show me the direction
That is appropriate to my vision.
*(Hilary and Romanus exit on the right. Capesius and Felix Bald
enter from the left, the Secretary leads them into the room.)*

SECRETARY:

I had thought Benedictus would return from
His trip today, but at the moment
He's not yet here; if you would try again tomorrow,
You'd certainly be able to see him then.

FELIX BALD:

Well, may we speak with our friend Hilary?

SECRETARY:

I'll let him know you'd like to see him.
(Secretary exits.)

FELIX BALD:

> What you experienced is truly of deep significance.
> Couldn't you repeat what you just said again?
> One can only correctly assess these things
> When one takes hold of them in spirit quite exactly.

CAPESIUS:

> It was this morning, just when I could believe
> Myself approaching the mystic mood of soul;
> The senses were silent; memory, too, silent.
> I lived only awaiting what would happen in spirit.
> First came about what is well known to me.
> Then, however, Strader's soul stood quite clearly
> Within my spirit vision. At first he didn't speak.
> I had time to reflect upon my own awakeness,
> But soon I also heard his words quite clearly.
> "Don't distance yourself from the true mystic mood."
> So it rang out, as if from his soul depths.
> Then he said, sharply emphasizing every word:
> "Striving for nothing – simply being peacefully still –
> The inner state of the soul totally expectation – –
> This is the mystic mood. – It awakens its self –
> Quite unsought for within the stream of life if
> The human soul has correctly strengthened itself –
> When it spiritually seeks with powerful thoughts.
> Often the mood comes at calm moments,
> But also in the storm of deeds; only then, it
> Wants the soul not to draw back thoughtlessly from
> The delicate vision of what is happening in spirit."

FELIX BALD:

> This almost sounds like an echo of my own words –
> Yet not with the full meaning of them.

CAPESIUS:

    If one really thought about it, one might
    Even find the opposite sense to your words –
    And one comes especially close to this interpretation
    When one considers what he went on to say:
    "Whoever awakens the mystic mood artificially though,
    Only leads their inner nature into *their self*;
    Indeed, in front of the realm of light they weave for
    Themselves the darkness of their own soul activity.
    Whoever wishes to seek this through mysticism,
    Kills their own vision with mystical delusion."

FELIX BALD:

    This can be nothing less than my own words,
    Turned round through Strader's spiritual approach,
    Ringing back within you as harmful mystic error.

CAPESIUS:

    Also though, Strader's last words were these:
    "Human beings cannot find the spirit world
    If they want to unlock it through seeking.
    Truth will not ring out within those souls
    Who over many years seek only a mood."
    (Philia appears, perceptible only to Capesius; Felix Bald shows
    by his stance that he doesn't comprehend the following.)

PHILIA:

    Capesius, if you will now pay heed to what,
    All unsought for in your seeking, you're being shown,
    Its light of many colors will strengthen you;
    It will pervade you as an image that has being
    Because your soul forces are revealing it to you.
    What the Sun being in your self is raying out,

Will diffuse Saturn's matured wisdom for you. It
Will then disclose itself to your vision, which you,
As earthly human being, will be able to comprehend.
I myself will then guide you to the Guardian
Who maintains his watch at the spirit Threshold. –

FELIX BALD:

Words are sounding forth from circles strange to me,
But no shining existence is producing these sounds
So for me they cannot be fully there as being.

CAPESIUS:

The instruction Philia is giving me
Is to guide me in future in such a way that
What I can already as an earthly individual
Find comprehensible within the circuit of my life
May also be revealed to me in spirit.

(Curtain falls.)

The same room as in the previous scene. At the beginning of the
scene Hilary's Wife in conversation with the Office Manager.

HILARY'S WIFE

As if destiny itself didn't want this deed
That my husband nonetheless deems necessary;
So it almost seems – just think how entangled
Are the threads this power has spun into the knot
Now completely encompassing our lives.

OFFICE MANAGER:

Into a knot of destiny that can at first
Seem truly unsolvable for human reason. –
- - - - - - - - - -
So it will certainly have to be cut. –
- - - - - - - - - -
I see no other possibility than that
There is now a break between your husband
And the present circle of my life. – –

HILARY'S WIFE:

Separate from you – never would my husband do that; –
It would contradict the spirit of the firm
Still preserved from his dear father
And which the son wishes loyally to hold to.

OFFICE MANAGER:

Is not then this loyalty already broken?
The goals Hilary is setting for himself
Certainly don't lie in the direction
That spirit always wanted to take.

HILARY'S WIFE:

> My husband's happiness in life is now
> Totally bound up with the success of this goal.
> I saw how his soul was transformed soon after
> It came to birth in a flash of thought within him. –
> Life had brought him only bleak soul desolation,
> Which he himself had carefully hidden
> From his closest circle of friends and which
> Thus even more sapped his strength from within.
> Previously he'd found himself empty because thoughts
> Which could have shown him the value of his life
> Didn't seem to want to germinate in his soul.
> When this plan for mystic activity
> Came before his soul, he was rejuvenated,
> Another man, always happy; – with this goal,
> He first felt the worth of his own life. – –
> That you could set yourself against him was the
> Farthest thing from his mind till he saw it happen.
> Then it hit him as hardly any blow
> Had ever hit him previously in his life.
> Oh, if you knew what he suffers through you,
> You would certainly moderate your hard stand.

OFFICE MANAGER:

> To go against my own convictions
> Would make it seem as if my human worth
> Were being lost. – To see Strader
> Placed at my side will be oppressive,
> However I've decided to bear this burden
> Because Romanus supports it, who I now understand
> Ever since he spoke to me about Strader.
> What he could say is for me
> The beginning of my own spirit pupilship.
> From his words flamed up a force

That entered actively into my soul;
I had never felt it previously.
His counsel is important to me, even when
I can't yet follow it with my understanding.
Romanus alone is now interceding for Strader;
The participation of the other Mystics in the work
Seems to him to be not only a hindrance to it,
He holds it as dangerous for the Mystics themselves.
For me, Romanus's opinion carries so *much* weight
I'm now forced to believe if Strader
Can't find his way to this deed without his friends,
It would be a sign of destiny for him. It would
Show he ought to first remain at the side
Of his friends and only later, out of his own mystical
Striving, create the impulse for the outer deed.
The fact that recently he stands much closer to
Those friends than formerly, when for a short while
They were quite estranged from him, makes me
Believe he will find himself in this situation
Even if he does see his goal as lost for the moment.

HILARY'S WIFE:

You see this man only with the eyes
Romanus has been able to open for you.
You should try to look at him impartially.
He can give himself over to spirit life in such a way
He seems to be totally withdrawn from the earth.
Then the spirit is fully present for him.
Theodora is then still living for him.
When speaking with him, it's as if one also had *her*
Standing by. Many Mystics can quite well form
The spirit message into words
That create conviction when thought about;

What Strader speaks is active in the speaking itself.
One can see he holds mere inner spiritual experience,
Which finds itself soon satisfied with feelings,
As of only little worth; as a Mystic he always
Gives the lead to his impulse for research.
That's also why he doesn't get the sense for science
That shows itself of practical service in life
Tangled up through mysticism. – Do try to see
This about him, and then also learn through him
That one may have to value his own judgement
About his friends more than that one
Romanus has been able to reach for himself.

OFFICE MANAGER:

For me, in this situation, which lies
Very far from my usual sphere of thinking,
The judgement of Romanus is like firm ground
On which I can stand. – If I were to give myself up
To a realm that brought me closer to mysticism,
I'd really need such guidance
As can only be offered by a person
Who could win my trust through what I could
Fully understand about their being.
(The Secretary enters.)

OFFICE MANAGER:

You arrive upset, my friend, what's happened?

SECRETARY *(hesitantly)*:

Doctor Strader has died just an hour or so ago.

OFFICE MANAGER:

Strader has died?

528

HILARY'S WIFE:

           Strader dead! – Where is
Hilary?

SECRETARY:

He's in his room …
As if he's been wounded by this message
Someone just now brought from Strader's home.
(Hilary's Wife exits, the Secretary follows her.)

OFFICE MANAGER *(alone)*:

Strader has died! Is this reality?

- - - - - - - - - -

Does spirit sleep, of which I've heard so much,
Now touch me? – The Powers of Destiny that here
Guide our threads display an earnest visage.
Oh, my little soul, what force is
Now completely grasping your thread of destiny
So it has a part to play within this knot?

- - - - - - - - - -

What must happen, will happen!

- - - - - - - - - -

Why have these words not left me
Ever since the moment Strader first spoke them
Before Hilary and I?
As if they had come to him from another world,
So they rang out; – spoken as if spirit enraptured! –
What should have happened? – I do, indeed,
Feel the spirit world took hold of me then.
In these words – its language rings out; –
How can I learn to understand it?

(The curtain falls.)

SCENE FIFTEEN

The same room as in the previous scene. Doctor Strader's Nurse is sitting there waiting. After the curtain has risen, the Secretary enters the room; later Benedictus. Ahriman.

SECRETARY

Benedictus will certainly appear soon
To receive the message from you himself. —
He's been away, he only just now returned.
He was a very great man, that Doctor Strader.
To begin with, I had no real confidence
In the tremendous plan Hilary had for our work,
But often when I was present as Strader
Showed him what was necessary for the work,
Every one of my objections quickly lost its force.
Always intelligent and with the strongest sense °
For what would be possible and also attainable,
Yet always endeavoring to find his ultimate goal
In a sensible way from out of the matter itself,
Not presuming anything in thinking beforehand.
The man acted quite in accord with mystic ways.
Just as people do who want to look on
The splendor of a view from a mountain peak.
They wait until they've reached the top,
They don't think up a picture in advance.

NURSE:

Within the stream of life, you got to know
A man of great gifts and strong spirit.
Within the short time I was permitted
To carry out the last earthly services for him,

I could but wonder at his lofty soul.
That dear soul, that apart from
Seven years of exceptional happiness,
Passed through his earthly life always alone.
The Mystics offered him wisdom.
He had need of love; – his desire for deeds,
That was really love – a love that creates many
Forms for itself in life in order to reveal itself.
What that soul sought in a mystical way was needed
By the noble fire of its being, just as is the peace
Of sleep by the body after periods of creating.

SECRETARY:

For him, the mystic wisdom was also the source
Of all creating – with him, everything was always
Completely filled by it but in the finest sense.

NURSE:

Because it was his very nature to always love
And to unite his soul with everything
Wanting to become a content of his life.
His last thoughts were ever about the work
He had dedicated himself to with love. – –
Strader's soul departed from its earthly work,
To which its love belonged,
Just as a person separates from a loved one.

SECRETARY:

Yet he lived in the spirit almost like a being,
And Theodora always stood livingly before him; –
That's what true mystic souls experience.

NURSE:

Because solitude united her with him.

531

Even in death she still stood before him. – By her,
Called to the spirit worlds for the completion
Of his work, so did he seem to himself.
A few hours before he died he wrote
These words for Benedictus I must now
Hand over to the Mystics' guide.
- - - - - - - - - -

So must life in our times unfold on earth,
Full of riddles – yet ever brightened
By Sun individuals of his kind,
From whom others, according to their planet,
May receive the light that awakens life.
(Benedictus enters the room; the Secretary leaves.)

NURSE:

Before his forces had grown too weak,
Strader wrote these few lines.
I am to give them over to his mystic friend.

BENEDICTUS:

And when he had written these words down,
Where did his soul dwell at the last?

NURSE:

At first, his life's latest plans were still
Alive in his thinking, then Theodora was united
With him in spirit; feeling that,
His soul gently wrested itself free of its sheath.

BENEDICTUS:

Have thanks, O loyal friend, for the service
You have just performed for him on earth.
(The Nurse exits. Benedictus reads the last words of Strader.)

"My friend, when I saw myself almost crushed,
Recognizing the opposition to my creating
Was not produced solely from outside,
That an inner fault in my foundation thought had
Hinderingly placed itself in the way of my work,
I beheld again that picture of which I spoke
To you a short while ago. Yet the outcome of
The picture had now become different. It was not
Ahriman who stood as a fighter over against me;
In his place appeared a spirit messenger
Whose figure presented itself in a way clearly
To be felt as my own error-filled thinking.
Then I was moved to remember those words
You had spoken about strengthening
The power of my soul forces. Thereupon,
That spirit messenger immediately disappeared. –"
Still a few words follow – I'm not capable
Of reading them – a chaos is spreading and
Actively weaving a veil of thoughts over them.
(Ahriman appears; Benedictus sees him.)
Who are you that like a shade brings itself to life
Out of this chaos within the circle of my soul?

AHRIMAN *(to himself)*:

He can certainly see me but not know me just yet,
So he won't now bring me that frightful pain
If I want to be active at his side.
(To Benedictus.)
I can inform you further of what Strader wanted
To entrust to you for your own benefit
And also for the mystic path of your pupils.

BENEDICTUS:

My mystic circle will always know itself

As bound to Strader's soul, even if sense existence
No longer creates the bridge between us;
But if a spirit messenger wills to approach us,
Revealing itself from out of its own worlds,
Then it must first of all gain our trust. –
It can only do so if it's willing to establish itself
As fully recognizable for our spirit vision.

AHRIMAN:

You're still only striving for self-knowledge.
In that case, an unknown spirit existence,
Which wanted to prove itself of service to you,
Were it to be allowed to stand at your side
Only when *recognized*, would first of all
Have to give itself over as a part to your self.

BENEDICTUS:

Whoever you may be, you only serve the Good
If you yourself don't will to strive within yourself,
If you're willing to lose yourself in human thinking
And thus arise anew in cosmic development.

AHRIMAN:

It's high time I got myself out of his circle
As quick as possible, for as soon as his vision
Can also *think* me in my true nature,
There'll soon be created within his thinking
A part of the force that'll slowly destroy me.
(Ahriman disappears.)

BENEDICTUS:

Only now do I recognize Ahriman, who here
Flees himself but yet creates thought-like
Tidings of his being within my self.
He strives to confuse human thinking

Because through an old inherited error
He seeks in it the sources of his own sufferings.
As yet, he does not know redemption will only
Be possible for him in future when he finds
His being again in the mirror of this thinking.
Thus he really does show himself to human beings
But not as he truly feels himself to be.
Revealing himself, yet also concealing himself,
He sought here to make use in his own manner
Of that fortuitous moment with Strader.
Through him, he also wanted to get at his friends;
But he will not be able to cover up his being
From the pupils of my mystic work in future. –
In wakefulness, they will also be able to think him
When he holds sway within their vision. – –
When he has to reveal himself to human souls,
They will be able to interpret the many forms
That seek to hide him.

But you, Sun-ripened soul of Strader, since
Through the strengthening of your spirit forces
You have compelled the messenger of error to be gone,
You shall shine as spirit star upon our friends;
With your light, you will always irradiate
Maria's and Johannes's existence in future;
Thus through you, they'll be able to arm themselves
Even more strongly for their spirit work,
And then through powerful thoughts as well,
Create themselves as revealers of soul light
When dark Ahriman, dampening down wisdom,
Wishes to spread the darkness of chaos
Over fully awakened spirit vision.

(Curtain falls.)

The title **The Souls Awakening** is meant to direct the reader towards how we have arrived, and can yet again in the future arrive, at a personal, inner, intellectual and moral state of awakeness. How is it that we are 'awake'? Without a spiritual view into our past lives or Karma, which our society does not have, it is almost impossible to fathom what past civilizations had for mental awakeness or moral uprightness among their citizens; we can see only the outward signs of it. But the burning question for our times is, how did we develop our present state of awakeness from one quite different back then? How do we grow in our intellectual, emotional, moral quality of consciousness, not just in the quantity? How should we develop a new inner state which will be suitable for our difficult future in order that we may be real, 'full' human beings?

Rudolf Steiner's Mystery Dramas may also be seen as pointing us to the factors and pathways by which we are able to actively take our own consciousness in hand, and these factors and pathways often lead us to other people. Our consciousness is a human matter, not to do with the animals, the plants, the minerals, even though it is with these we fill it. It is from human beings we learn as children and develop an adult mentality, and in this way have developed the consciousness which is the norm in our present civilization. There have certainly been great explorers and adventurers, military leaders and statesmen we look up to, but the effect our mother or sister had upon us might be far greater. Those effects are not seen, spoken of, nor 'proven', but our consciousness is real.

Awakening to the question of where we got a particular aspect of our consciousness, must lead us on to fathoming our real inner relationships with other states of consciousness, other human beings. And then we may see, that we owe another for the fact that we have an ability or a particular content of our consciousness. Such an investigation will lead us into a whole stream of changing, growing, developing consciousnesses which have been the history of human culture and civilization. The other surprising thing we find is that there are, indeed, certain individuals who were and are able to survey and work with these streams of consciousnesses, moulding, influencing, and furthering them. Such individuals may never be seen or known in our outer civilization, but they are undoubtably there, just as the explorers or generals are.

The scenes (**5** and **6**) in the spirit domain and the scenes (**7** and **8**) showing an Egyptian temple ceremony, both present other states of consciousness than those current in mainstream society. They are not to be thought of as symbolical but as quite concrete realities. The only thing is, in order to be able to fully fathom these concrete realities, another state of consciousness needs to be developed, and so it is just by working with these dramas and these scenes that one of those individuals who knows the true states of consciousness in their actual developmental streams, can teach us to open ourselves and develop still another state.

The translation of particular words needs clarification:

"Wort/Worte" which mean 'word/words' in English, have a special problem. In German the singular form is often used for what would be a plural usage in English. This can usually be handled in the translation, but there is one case that is always difficult, and that is with World Word, Cosmic Word, Holy Word, or Word of God We use the singular here, too, but when exactly the German is referring to the Cosmic Word or simply to cosmic words is often interpretive and still more often with Rudolf Steiner probably both. The reader must keep an eye out and be ever ready to try the alternative when 'word' appears in a larger connection.

"Schein" normally means 'appearance' or 'outer shine' and is usually connected with sense perception. For Rudolf Steiner, however, it is also used with regard to what appears to us when we can see at a certain stage of the spiritual world. There it also has this sense of what is 'shining for us' but now as a reality, so shining as a glorious light or radiance. This has also been called in the past, 'glory', which is used in the bible (the glory of the Lord) among other places. I have kept the word 'shine' or 'shining' throughout, leaving the reader to decide when exactly the spiritual shine is intended.

Mention should be made here of the book "A Commentary on Rudolf Steiner's Four Mystery Plays" by Harry Collison. While it is long out of print, it does contain important insights on the dramas by one who worked with Rudolf Steiner on the original production of the plays. A few points in the Notes have been drawn from this book.

The original diagrams made by Rudolf Steiner for the covers of the four Mystery Dramas as first published have been developed for this edition based on the work of Bertha Meyer-Jacobs who created the same diagrams into jewelery brooches.

Page

403   Rudolf Steiner is reported to have calculated that
Johannes would be about 65 years old at the beginning of
this drama.

     Hilary's, the German word is <Gottgetreu>, i.e., Hilary's
last name, True-to-God; but it does not indicate if the
person or the firm, which also could have this name, is
being referred to. I have used Hilary throughout pages
403, 404 and once on 412 as an easier and more satisfying
name for a firm, but the reader must realize it may be the
'boss' alone who is being referred to by his second name,
or it may be the firm is being spoken of.

     in a not all too new style, this could perhaps mean in the
somewhat rough style of a lumber mill, as opposed to
simply an old-fashioned style.

405   *I'll thus ... on it*, this sentence may have alternate meanings:
I'll add to the dead physical thing (i.e., the product),
Which is something it does seem to me to be our job to
do, (or: which our work does seem to me to be all about)
The soul, which first gives it its sense (meaning/mind).

     Such marvelous creating, alternatively; magical creating.

406   *Unthinkingly give ... to give it*; this part of the sentence
seems to be unclear and may refer both to one item of
production as well as to one person in life.

     spirit, or 'mind' here and following on to **407**. There
seems to be a double play in German not exactly possible
in English, and which may perhaps include a confusion
between Hilary and the Office Manager about what they
are really talking about, i.e., spirit or mind.

411   *spirit*, or mind, as with **406, 407**.

     mirage, <Luftgebilde> literally: air formation.

     outing, <Ausgang>, this may be understood as an outing
to look at the new 'site', it may also be simply a tour/
inspection tour of the factory itself.

418   *what the gods feel*, see Note p. **309**.

425   *that other one*, there could be a double meaning here, i.e.
Capesius, or the other part of his own soul.

426   *to spirit individuality*, perhaps 'essentiality'; the German is:
<Geisteswesenheit>.

     demons, see Note p. **36**.

449   *supremely happy in the thought*, this may refer to Mrs. Bald herself or perhaps to the Fairy Tale Beings.

451   *When such spirits...*, alternatively:
When mystics make alliance with beings
That submissively serve their spirit mood,
Then those good spirits turn away from them.
The meaning of ..., the reference in this passage is unclear; it could be either 'it' or 'he', i.e., the spirit of the father or the father of Hilary himself, throughout.

462   *you*, could be either Maria or Benedictus.

469   *circle of my sight*, for materialistic seeing we would say 'horizon of my sight', but this has to do with the soul and its ability to see/perceive in the spiritual world, thus circle may be more justified here, although also sphere.

478   *penitent*, is clearly feminine in the German and is referring to The Soul of Mrs. Bald.
the Daemons are longing for your work, here I believe not demons, rather spiritual beings, which may be nature beings or the spiritual entity of human beings in the spiritual world, are meant. *their*, may refer to the 'souls' or the daemons themselves, see Note p. 36.

479   *We will reach the spirit circle of his soul.* i.e., Johnnes; but this sentence may also be meant in a purely impersonal way:
We will reach the spirit circle of the soul.

484   *Third Cultural Epoch of the earth*, 2907 – 747 BC; also call the Babylonian-Egyptian-Hebrew Epoch.
Threshold Guardian, the name is here, as in German, changed around to indicate the person who represents the Guardian of the Threshold in this Egyptian ritual.
One could see him as spirit enraptured, it's possible to interpret this as that 'one can see him sometime spirit enraptured', however I do not think this would fit with the lines on the next page where the Hierophant then asks if the Mystic has indeed seen him in this state.

486   *fog*, or 'hazy cloud' as translated earlier, see p. 467ff & 515ff.

489   *spirit insight*, it may be this should be read 'spiritual intuition' instead.

490   H. Collison gives the following arrangement for this scene:

Most High Hierophant

Keeper of the Words   Hierophant

Threshold Guardian   The Mystic

Neophyte

ALTAR

Keeper of the Seals

Rep. of Water   Rep. of Earth

Rep. of Fire   Rep. of Air

Philia Astrid Luna The Other Philia

2 Priests   2 Priests

Ahriman   Lucifer

as sphinx   as sphinx

There are indications from Rudolf Steiner's lectures he may have seen this scene as having taken place about 1322 BC. Collison says Rudolf Steiner reported that in fashioning the words and actions of the Hierophant, he had in mind Akhnaton, the Egptian Pharoah who broke with the old form of religion and turned to a religion of one god only.

490   *shining web of semblance*, <Scheingewebe>, means on the one hand woven material that is not real but an appearance, a chimera, on the other hand, something shining, glancing, that is seen as very beautiful.

495   *butterflies*, or 'moths'.

501   *density*, German <Dichte?.

502/503 *lap*, or 'womb'.

505   *interest*, or 'sympathy'; German <Anteil>.

514   *left-over junk of a being*, German <Wesenszeug>.

515   *something spun in the brain*, German <Hirngespinst>.
        Do you know Doctor Strader, who serves me? Compare Goethe's **Faust**, Prologue in Heaven, line 299:
        Do you know Faust, <The Doctor> My servant!

516   *too crafty*, or 'over-crafty' in the sense of superfluous, or 'super-crafty'
        You reason so well a person can even hear you, or 'You reason so well a person can actually listen to you!'

518   *bright*, means here 'daylight brightness'.

520   *all too clever*, as in **516**.

530   *intelligent*, possibly 'wise', or literally: full of spirit.

ISBN 1-41205005-7

9 781412 050050